RAYMOND WILLIAMS was born on 31 August 1921 in the Welsh border village of Pandy. He was educated at the village school, at Abergavenny Grammar, and at Trinity College, Cambridge. After active service in the war, he worked as an adult education tutor in the Oxford University Delegacy for Extra-mural Studies until 1961, when he was elected Fellow of Jesus College, Cambridge, where he was Professor of Drama from 1974 to 1983, and where he taught until his death in 1990.

In 1947 he part-edited *Politics and Letters*, to which George Orwell contributed. Williams' other studies include *Drama in Performance* (1954), *Culture and Society 1780-1950* (1958), *The Long Revolution* (1961), *Modern Tragedy* (1966), *Drama from Ibsen to Brecht* (1968), *The Country and the City* (1973), *Television: Technology and Cultural Form* (1974), *Keywords* (1976),*Marxism and Literature* (1977), *Culture* (1981), *Towards 2000* (1983), *Writing in Society* (1983), *Resources of Hope: Culture, Democracy, Socialism* (1989), *Writing, Culture and Politics* (1989), and*What I Came To Say* (1989). He was also the author of several novels, and was working on the third volume of his fictional trilogy about life in the Welsh Borders over the ages, *People of the Black Mountains*, when he died.

Modern Masters

Orwell

Raymond Williams

FontanaPress
An Imprint of HarperCollins*Publishers*

First published in Great Britain in 1971 by Fontana
Second Edition published in 1984 by Flamingo

This edition first issued in 1991 by Fontana Press,
an imprint of HarperCollins Publishers,
77–85 Fulham Palace Road,
Hammersmith, London W6 8JB

9 8 7 6 5 4 3 2 1

Printed and bound in Great Britain by
HarperCollins Book Manufacturing, Glasgow

Contents

1 Blair into Orwell

Eric Arthur Blair was born in 1903, at Motihari, in British-occupied India. He was the second child of Richard Walmesley Blair and Ida Mabel Limouzin. His father, then aged 46, was an agent in the Opium Department of the Indian Civil Service. His paternal grandfather had served in the Indian Army and later become an Anglican clergyman. His maternal grandfather had been a teak merchant in Burma and later a rice-grower.

When Eric Blair was four the family returned to England and settled at Henley, though the father worked in India until his retirement in 1912. Eric wrote later that he barely saw his father before he was eight. His mother, eighteen years younger than her husband, bore their third child in 1908. The family was then of two daughters and a son, born at five-year intervals.

At the age of eight, Eric Blair was sent to a private preparatory school in Sussex, and lived there, except in the school holidays, until he was thirteen. He then went by scholarship to two private secondary schools: Wellington (for one term); Eton (for four and a half years). He again lived in the schools, except during holidays. When he left Eton, the family moved from Oxfordshire to Suffolk. Eric Blair joined the Indian Imperial Police and was trained in Burma. He served there for nearly five years and then in 1927, while home on leave, decided not to return. His resignation from the Imperial Police became effective on the first day of 1928.

Blair's life until he was twenty-four is in all its visible

details a training for membership in the administrative middle class of imperialist Britain. His family, on both sides, had lived and worked in India and Burma, in the army, administration, and trade. His first adult work was directly within this pattern. He had, moreover, grown up with that characteristic absence of normal family life, in an England which was primarily a home base and a network of ruling-class schools. When this pattern was broken, in 1927, he found himself in an England where he had spent two-thirds of his life but always within institutions or, more rarely, in a family situation, which defined a particular set of social relationships. The political and cultural dominance of men with similar backgrounds and histories has been so marked, in the first half of the twentieth century in Britain, that Blair's growing-up has been commonly described as normal and orthodox. In any other terms, including those of the lives of most people in Britain, it was in important ways strange and even alien. This needs to be remembered and emphasised as we look at the next nine years of his life. For what these amounted to were the making of a new set of social relationships and the creation, in an important sense, of a new social identity. This is the critical evolution of Blair into Orwell.

The reasons for the first break are undoubtedly complex, but two factors are evident. Blair had been clear, in his adolescence, that he wanted to become a writer. The Imperial Police was in this and other respects what he called an unsuitable profession. But there is also good evidence (though mainly from much later, when his mind had cleared) that he had come to understand and reject the imperialism he was serving. Imperialism, he wrote, at the end of his change, was an evil thing, and the sooner he chucked his job and got out of it the better

(CEJL, I, 236). Yet within its service his response was more complicated. He was stuck, as he later saw it, between hatred of the Empire he was serving and rage against the native people who opposed it and made his immediate job difficult. Theoretically, he says, he was all for the Burmese and all against their British oppressors. Practically he was at once opposed to the dirty work of imperialism and involved in it.

Some parts of this complex response can be seen as continuing through the rest of his life. Yet what is also crucial, at the time of the break, is his uncertain and ambiguous relationship to England: the society he knows and belongs to, yet in other ways, except in abstraction, does not know at all. Thus it would have been possible for him to leave the Imperial Police and settle in England within the same class network. If he had been reacting only against explicit imperialism, this might have been a normal course. But the problem of relationship within England was even more critical. What Blair actually did, in the first six months of his release, was to go on what he thought of as an expedition to the East End of London, to get to know the English poor. He took as a base a room in Notting Hill. Then, in the spring of 1928, he took a room in a working-class district of Paris. His favourite aunt, Nellie Limouzin, had lived in the same road in Notting Hill and was living in Paris for the eighteen months of his stay there. The expedition to the East End was of a kind which he was later often to repeat: a journey of discovery of ordinary English people. But taking those first two-and-a-half years of his new life as a whole, it is reasonable to see his main impulse as his establishment as a writer. For that purpose the choice of Paris was characteristic of the time. Ten years later, he wrote that Paris in the late 1920s was 'invaded by such a swarm of artists, writers, students, dilettanti, sight-seers, debauchees, and plain idlers as the world has never seen ... in some quarters of the town the so-called artists must actually have outnumbered the working population'. Then 'the slump descended like another Ice Age, the cosmopolitan mob of artists vanished' (CEJL, I, 493). We must notice the habit, characteristic of several phases of his experience, of writing in these contemptuous and devaluing terms of something of which he had himself been a part. He wrote two novels, which have been lost, during his time in Paris, and published some articles in French and English. He became ill with pneumonia, worked ten weeks as a dishwasher and kitchen porter, and then returned to England at the end of 1929.

For the next two and a half years he worked to establish himself as a writer from a different base. He used his parents' home in Suffolk for writing and earned money from occasional articles and teaching. He completed several versions of what was to become his first book, called, not by his choice, *Down and Out in Paris and London*. 'I would *rather* answer to "dishwasher" than "down and out" ' (CEJL, I, 107). The book was a record of his experiences, but 'if it is all the same to everybody I would prefer [it] to be published pseudonymously'. Since he was earning his living as a teacher when it was due to be published, one aspect of this preference is understandable. But the question of a name, and the deeper question of an identity, had arisen before. He was still going on what he thought of as expeditions in England : living with tramps, with hop-pickers, and in working-class districts. Discussing the publication of *Down and Out in Paris and London*, he wrote to his agent in late 1932 :

As to a pseudonym, a name I always use when tramp-
ing etc is P. S. Burton, but if you don't think this
sounds a probable kind of name, what about
>Kenneth Miles
>George Orwell
>H. Lewis Allways.
I rather favour George Orwell.   (CEJL, I, 106)

The Orwell is a river in Suffolk, south of his parents'
home.

This first book by Orwell was published in 1933. During the next three years he completed his establishment
as a writer. He earned money from teaching, working in
a bookshop, and reviewing, and began living for longer
periods away from his parents' home. *Down and Out in
Paris and London* was followed by the novel *Burmese
Days*, published first in the United States rather than in
England because of his English publisher's fear of its giv-
ing offence in Burma. Then came two more novels, *A
Clergyman's Daughter*, published in 1935, and *Keep the
Aspidistra Flying*, published in 1936. In the Spring of
1936 he moved to a village store at Wallington, in Hert-
fordshire, and two months later married Eileen O'Shaugh-
nessy, daughter of a customs collector, an Oxford graduate (1927) in English, a teacher and journalist, and later
(1934) a London graduate student in psychology. They
were Eric and Eileen Blair, but the recognisable identity
of George Orwell had now, after the years of difficulty
and transition, been clearly established.

Orwell's reputation at this time, as writer and journalist, was based mainly on his accounts of poverty and
depression. His expeditions and then his convincing reports had given him a particular though limited identity
in the literary world. He had first broken his orthodox

social relationships and then, for irregular periods but consciously and recurrently, dropped out of them. What he brought back, into a class-conscious culture and at a time of general poverty and depression, were reports from a world that seemed as distant in experience as Burma. His next book was a commission in this precise identity: an inquiry, for the Left Book Club, into the life of the poor and unemployed.

But 1936, when he received this commission, was a year of crisis and change in a quite different dimension. While the commission prolonged his previous identity as a writer, his way of fulfilling it, in *The Road to Wigan Pier*, marked an entry to a new project, as a political writer, which was to last the rest of his life. For while the first part of the book is the kind of reporting that he had been asked for and that he could do so well, the second part is an essay on class and socialism which is effectively the first statement of Orwell's basic political position. Repeating his opposition to imperialism and the class system, he now adds a commitment to socialist definitions of freedom and equality while at the same time attacking most forms of the organised socialist movement and especially various kinds of English middle-class socialists.

He had made the journey to Lancashire and Yorkshire in February and March, before settling at Wallington and opening his shop in the afternoons. He was married in June, and during the summer and autumn wrote his book. But in July the Spanish civil war broke out, and by the end of the autumn Orwell was preparing to go to Spain, to collect material for articles, and perhaps to fight. Soon after he had arrived in Barcelona he joined the militia of the POUM (Partido Obrero de Unificacion Marxista), and was in action with them in January 1937.

He then transferred to the British Independent Labour Party contingent serving with the POUM militia, became a corporal and later a lieutenant, and was wounded in the middle of May. He had tried, in April, to join the International Brigade in Madrid, but became involved in the conflict between the Republican authorities and the POUM, and again, after his convalescence, was personally involved in this when the POUM was declared illegal. He got out into France in June.

This experience of war and revolutionary politics hardened his position in several ways. It did not make him an anti-communist, since he had rejected Soviet-style communism as a possible commitment many years before. Yet he had tried to join the International Brigade, in the crisis of Spain, and it was mainly his direct experience of Communist–POUM rivalry that sharpened his anti-communism to a positive position. At the same time he became, for the next two or three years, a revolutionary socialist. *The Road to Wigan Pier*, in which he had attacked most orthodox British socialist positions, including what he knew as Marxism, had been published in March 1937 while he was at the front. As soon as he returned from Spain, he began writing *Homage to Catalonia*, which completed his break with the orthodox Left. The book was published in April 1938, and in June Orwell joined the Independent Labour Party, in which he stayed until the early months of the war. He wanted to go to India to write a new book, but he became ill with tuberculosis in the late winter of 1938 and was in a sanatorium until the late summer. With a loan from L. H. Myers (author of *The Near and the Far*) he then went to spend the winter in Morocco, returning to England in the spring of 1939.

During the winter in Morocco he wrote his fourth

novel, *Coming Up for Air*. On his return to England he wrote some of his best-known essays: on Dickens, on Boys' Weeklies, and, as war was beginning, 'Inside the Whale'. From Morocco he had been writing letters sketching the possibility of an underground anti-war Left, as the only alternative to a slow drift into fascism in Britain. But when war began, he came to believe that 'now we are in this bloody war we have got to win it and I would like to lend a hand' (CEJL, I, 410). He was rejected by the army as physically unfit, and was again short of money as opportunities for occasional journalism declined. He moved back to London in May 1940, and in the autumn of that year wrote 'The Lion and the Unicorn', an essay subtitled 'Socialism and the English Genius'. From early 1941 he began writing 'London Letters' for the American *Partisan Review*, and then in August joined the BBC as a talks producer in the Indian section of the Eastern Service, where he stayed until late 1943. He served for a time in the Home Guard and as a firewatcher.

The year 1943 was in several ways a turning-point. In March Orwell's mother died. He had to leave the Home Guard because he was ill, and he left the BBC to become literary editor of *Tribune*, then directed by Aneurin Bevan. He took on more regular book-reviewing, but the decisive event was that late in the year he began writing *Animal Farm*. It was complete by February 1944, but was rejected by several publishers on political grounds. It did not eventually appear until August 1945, at the end of the war.

Towards the end of the war in Europe, Orwell travelled to France and later to Germany and Austria as a reporter. He and his wife had adopted a son in 1944, but in March 1945 his wife died during an operation. He kept the child, and later in the year made his first journey to the island of Jura, off the Scottish coast. In 1946 he settled there, with his younger sister as housekeeper, though returning to London for the winter. His elder sister had died in 1946, and his own health was getting steadily worse. During 1947, in the early months of renewed tuberculosis, he wrote the first draft of *Nineteen Eighty-Four* and in 1948, amid several attacks, wrote the second draft. By the end of that year he was very seriously ill and was to write hardly anything else.

The extraordinary commercial success of *Animal Farm* was to end the financial worries from which he had suffered as a writer, since that time of decision, nearly twenty years earlier, when he left the Imperial Police. But by the time this had happened he was already into his last years of recurrent illness and pain. In September 1949 he went into hospital in London, and in October married Sonia Brownell. In January 1950 he died.

2 England whose England?

'England my England', wrote Lawrence. 'England your England', wrote Orwell.

Orwell wrote two long essays about England: 'The Lion and the Unicorn' in 1940, and 'The English People' in 1944. Near the beginning of each, he introduces the viewpoint of someone arriving in England. 'When you come back to England from any foreign country, you have immediately the sensation of breathing a different air' (CEJL, II, 57). 'It is worth trying for a moment to put oneself in the position of a foreign observer, new to England, but unprejudiced, and able because of his work to keep in touch with ordinary, useful, unspectacular people' (CEJL, III, 1). This may seem no more than a literary device. Much of Orwell's writing about England is so close and detailed, his emphasis on ordinary English virtues so persistent, that he is now often seen as the archetypal Englishman, the most native and English of writers. But it is necessary to remember the real history: the creation of Orwell from Blair. Many of the ways in which he sees England are affected and sometimes determined by his history: born, educated, and taking his first job in a ruling-class network that was in some deliberate ways cut off from ordinary England; rejecting this network and setting out on his own to discover the country for himself. Similarly, many of the ways in which he values English life are affected and determined by this kind of journey. His notable attachment to what he saw as ordinary England is an act not so much of membership as of conscious affiliation.

We shall see how this affected his deepest imagination and his values. But we need to look first at the England to which he was reacting in this special way. For there was one special advantage in his history : that he came to look at England within a knowledge of its Empire : a point of view on this insular society which was in many ways penetrating.

'Not Counting·Niggers', he wrote in 1939, about a plan for a Federal Union which was geographically similar (and hence politically similar) to what we now know as NATO and the Common Market. What was left out of the plan, in a convenient oversight, was the existence of a huge colonial population controlled by this bloc. 'What we always forget is that the overwhelming bulk of the British proletariat does not live in Britain but in Asia and Africa ... This is the system which we all live on' (CEJL, I, 397). And as he writes elsewhere : 'I was in the Indian Police five years, and by the end of that time I hated the imperialism I was serving with a bitterness which I probably cannot make clear. In the free air of England that kind of thing is not fully intelligible. In order to hate imperialism you have got to be part of it' (RWP, 145).

The eyes of the observer, of the man coming back to England, are eyes full of this experience of imperialism. But he is not coming to England in the same way as, say, an Indian or an African student : to a foreign country about which he has only read. He has been educated here; his family lives here. He is aware of the internal structure of English society, but from a class position which he has only theoretically rejected. At school, he said, he had had 'no notion that the working class were human beings. At a distance ... I could agonise over their sufferings, but I still hated them and despised them when I came anywhere near them ... To the shock-absorbers of the bourgeoisie, such as myself, "common people" still appeared brutal and repulsive' (RWP, 142–3).

This very special position, a kind of conscious double vision, is central to Orwell. It has been overlooked, time and again, by people reading back from his later reporting, and especially by people who shared his kind of childhood and education but who did not undergo his subsequent direct revulsion from imperialism. It is impossible to convince most people who had Orwell's kind of separated education that they are not, in the most central ways, English. For of course the definition of 'England', its myth and its ideology, has been for more than a century in just these hands. This is the class which does most of the writing, which directs not only its own but most other institutions, and which, travelling abroad, is known to most of the world as 'the English'. A world-view of England, we can fairly say, has been based on the character of this tiny minority.

Yet it is not, as a minority, without its internal differences. It is necessary to describe it as a ruling class, and at that time the ruling class of an empire. But only part of the class was quite wholly in command: able to live on its property and investments, or to move directly into the central metropolitan institutions. A much larger part had a harder and humbler function. Their education, essentially, was as servants of a system to which they belonged only as functionaries. And it was these people who went out to the edges of the system, facing its realities directly. Eric Blair was born into what he later called, in exactly this sense, the 'lower-upper-middle-class'. Theoretically a member of the ruling class, and sharing its insistent myth and ideology of 'England', he and men like him were in practice on the outer edge of the system, in several ways. Owning no land or substantial property, they were dependent on their professional salaries which were in turn dependent on accepting the definitions of 'profession' and 'service' which the system as a whole had created. Often, in such a group, there is a kind of overadjustment to the very myths which offer to define their membership in the class as a whole. The fear of dropping out of the class of which they are literally the bottom edge can produce more rigid and more blatant definitions of their 'England' than might be found at the relaxed and comfortable centre. Eric Blair's first appearance in print, at the age of eleven, was with a characteristic poem: 'Awake! Young Men of England'. It is a boy miming a country and a role.

Seen from outside, as most of us must now see it, this position generates a particular tension: that of the man who is simultaneously dominator and dominated. The tension can be overlaid by a miming rigidity that can come to serve as the whole personality. Or it can lead, as in Blair's case, to crisis: the crisis which made him into Orwell. And then the double vision, rooted in the simultaneous positions of dominator and dominated, is at once powerful and disturbed.

When he re-entered England, that is to say, his primary impulse was negative: a rejection of the system and the ideology in which he had been educated and in which he had served. But because of the character of the system, there was no other 'England' to which he could immediately go. He could only drop out of the one England and make expeditions to the other. When he summed all this up towards the end of his journey, what he had to say was affected as much by the character of the negation as by the character of the subsequent and conscious affiliation:

> I felt that I had got to escape not merely from imperialism but from every form of man's dominion over man. I wanted to submerge myself, to get right down among the oppressed, to be one of them and on their side against their tyrants ... It was in this way that my thoughts turned towards the English working class. It was the first time that I had ever been really aware of the working class, and to begin with it was only because they supplied an analogy. They were the symbolic victims of injustice, playing the same part in England as the Burmese played in Burma. (RWP, 149–50)

This, very clearly, and described with his usual frankness, is that form of *negative identification* in which approach and affiliation to a new group is a function of the subject's initial and formative social experience.

England, whose England? In *The Road to Wigan Pier* the sense of the journey is still active; Orwell is describing the 'two nations', discovering how (in that middle-class phrase) the 'other half' lives. He is at once compassionate and indignant, drawn and repelled. He is describing a country in which two-thirds of the population are working-class people at a time of depression and widespread unemployment. All his active arguments and images are of contrasts, intolerable contrasts. 'England', as any simple idea, has been destroyed by these contrasts. The single image of his childhood has been replaced by the particularities, the variations, the inequalities, of mine and mill, slum and council-house, caravan site and slagheap, teashop and Tudor villa. This is an active England, an England to move through.

The England of the later essays, written in wartime, is different. It is not necessarily more true or false, but it is again, in some significant ways, single: 'Economically, England is certainly two nations, if not three or four. But at the same time the vast majority of the people *feel* themselves to be a single nation and are conscious of resembling one another more than they resemble foreigners' (CEJL, II, 64). That, perhaps, is not very surprising. It would presumably be true of any long-settled country. But in and through this unexceptional observation, something else is being said.

> England is the most class-ridden country under the sun. It is a land of snobbery and privilege, ruled largely by the old and silly. But in any calculation about it one has got to take into account its emotional unity, the tendency of nearly all its inhabitants to feel alike and act together in moments of supreme crisis. (CEJL, II, 67)

The last clause of this passage, written in 1940 at a time of exceptional national unity under the threat of invasion, is more obviously acceptable than the preceding description of 'emotional unity', which makes a much larger claim. 'England is ... but ...' is the recurring pattern of this argument, leading to a particular climax which comes 'as near as one can ... to describing England in a phrase':

> a family with the wrong members in control.

Now Orwell was neither the first nor the last to say something like this. The statement's interest is in where it comes on the scale of his development. There is not much sense of a family or of emotional unity in the depressed and suffering England of *The Road to Wigan Pier*. The emphasis there is on the realities and consequences of a class society. What happens, I think, is that Orwell first moves through two phases of response to 'England': the myth of his boyhood—the special people, the 'family'—is succeeded by the observations of his return—a scene of bitter and bleak contradictions. But then, in a third phase, he creates a new myth which until quite recently has remained effective. Qualifying the original image with the facts of the economic and social inequality, he creates the sense of an England of basic ordinariness and decency, a 'real England', 'an everlasting animal stretching into the future and the past', in which it can be seen almost as an accident, or at least as an evident archaism, that the 'wrong members' of the family are in control.

Orwell's great influence since the 1940s owes as much to this powerful image as to any other single achievement. And it would not be so powerful if it did not contain some truth. Orwell's emphasis on the depth of civil liberties in Britain and on the feelings that support them is, in the world as he knew it and as we continue to know it, justified. His further emphasis on the gentleness and mildness of much ordinary English life, on these qualities being positive achievements in a world of killing and anger, is again reasonable. Certain kinds of informality, friendliness, and tolerance in much of everyday English life support his emphasis on 'decency' as a virtue. But it is possible to know and acknowledge all these things and still, in analysis, go either way.

Orwell is nearest to what I believe to be the truth when he describes these characteristics as part of a genuinely popular culture which 'must live to some extent *against* the existing order' (CEJL, II, 59). Or again when he speaks of a 'subtle network of compromises', of adjustments through which certain virtues, certain achievements, are maintained alongside certain evident and radical injustices. But as we begin to define in these ways, we find that we are discussing very complicated relationships within a very complicated social structure. Orwell recognises and emphasises the complexity, but he does not develop any kind of thinking which can sustain and extend a critical analysis of structures. The evidence is collected, often in sharp detail, and the sense of a climate, an atmosphere, is memorably created. But a social structure is not a climate. It can never be enough to say that certain virtues exist *alongside* certain injustices, as if they were contrasting facts of the natural world (on which, in his social imagery, Orwell so commonly draws). In a society, these facts are relationships of an active, historical, and developing kind. And it is this kind of reality which Orwell's image of England obscures.

That is a fact about his method. But, as so often, the method depends ultimately on a point of view. Orwell's way of describing the faults of this 'family' with the 'wrong members' in control has again been influential. Class, for example, is described mainly in terms of differences and snobberies in accent, clothes, tastes, furnishing, food. And this has become habitual. In *The Road to Wigan Pier* the sinking middle class, realising the identity of their interests with the exploited working class, would have 'nothing to lose but our aitches'. Correspondingly, in the milder world of 'The Lion and the Unicorn', the prosperous workers are becoming 'visibly ... more middle-class'. In this way of thinking Orwell prepared the orthodox political beliefs of a generation. For of course it is true that if class means only these differences in private social behaviour, differences that are often little more than external and trivial, a certain 'classlessness' is inevitable in conditions of growing prosperity and extended education and communications. The difference from the old overt and vulgar display of class distinction is something any reasonable person would welcome. But by keeping the definition of class to these characteristics, which any prosperous industrial society will in any case erode, another set of facts, in which class is a powerful and continuing economic relationship —as between the owners of property and capital and the owners only of labour and skill—is effectively masked.

For what is it, after all, which puts the 'wrong members of the family' in control? Is it only a deference to their accents, their clothes, their styles of eating and furnishing? It is strange to have to make this point about an Orwell whose emphasis on the determining fact of money is so intense and even at times (in the thirties) extreme. But there's money in the pocket, and more money in more pockets will mean precisely the classlessness he refers to. There's also, however, that quite different 'money' which is capital, which is the ownership and creation of the means of social life itself. Here any question about control is inevitably a question about this ownership, which can indeed remain unaltered in any major way during a period in which the visible signs of 'class', the small change of the system, have been if not wiped out (for there is no sign of that happening, thirty years after Orwell wrote) at least modified, moderated, and evolved.

The clearest sign of the weakness of Orwell's description—but also, as it happens, of its appeal—can be seen in his discussion of what he still calls the ruling class. Here his initial attitudes are complicated, for the reasons discussed earlier. He sees his own group, the service families, pushed down in importance by the growth of centralised bureaucracy and by the monopoly trading companies. Their vitality and initiative, he thinks, have declined since the high point of Empire in the years just before he was born. At the same time, a part of the same class has become not merely frustrated but disaffected. This is his regular description of English middle-class intellectuals, especially Left intellectuals: shallow, negative, and out of touch with and against their own country.

But these he sees as the outriders: in the ruling-class family but now either as its servants or as its black sheep. The core of the ruling class is still there, and what is most remarkable about it, he says, is its stupidity. In terms of the family that is England, these are the 'irresponsible uncles and bedridden aunts'. The image, as it happens, admits no father.

It is a beguiling picture. What happened in the ruling class, according to Orwell, was a decay of ability. Their position 'had long ceased to be justifiable'. An 'aristocracy constantly recruited from parvenus ... there they sat, at the centre of a vast empire and a world-wide financial network, drawing interest and profits and spending them—on what?' On nothing useful, to be sure. 'Only half a million people, the people in the country houses, definitely benefitted from the existing system' (CEJL, II, 69–70). True enough, but what is remarkable is that this is seen as the 'decay' of a ruling class, as if that gang of aristocrats recruited from parvenus had *ever* had any different or more justifiable social aims. And the only real test of their 'ability' would be, surely, their capacity to continue to impose themselves.

It is much easier to despise the ruling class than to hate and break them. Orwell's comic uncles and aunts are a recurring radical image, but to see the actual ruling class in that way is in the end an indulgence, dependent emotionally on that very middle-class image of England as a family. Once again, the naïve myth has been qualified by some of its unacknowledged consequences and then, in a more acceptable form, in part restored. 'Long ceased to be justifiable'—that presupposes an original justification, when the aristocracy was not bumbling and stupid but able, daring, and ruthless. It is a radical illusion and a radical rhetoric which in its sentimental and indulgent underestimate has always weakened the British Left. Orwell was nearer to the facts of the society he was observing, and nearer to the necessary response to them, when he wrote, with an anger he usually reserved for his enemies on the Left, of 'the rat-trap faces of bankers and the brassy laughter of stockbrokers', against which all social criticism broke.

The difficulty, surely, lies in the original image of a family. Orwell hated what he saw of the consequences of capitalism, but he was never able to see it, fully, as an economic and political *system*. His great strength in personalising particular injustices was not supported by any adequate understanding of the very general forces involved. He wanted, deeply and genuinely, to bring 'the real England' to the surface, to turn the war into 'a revolutionary war', both defeating fascism and finishing capitalism. In part this programme is the understandable rhetoric of 1940, and it was quite widely shared throughout the war years. But inside it there is a special view of the system that is being opposed: an influential view, right through to the Labour governments of the sixties, which has now shown its inadequacy. The old system, with its aristocratic and parvenu stupidities, is seen as a top layer, to be replaced with 'new blood, new men, new ideas'. The spread of the middle-class is seen as having made the old class analysis almost obsolete, and the working-class anyway is believed to be rapidly acquiring middle-class habits and ideas. The ruling class is seen as having become mere owners, their work done for them by managers and technicians. All that is then needed, it seems, is for all the decent members of the family—middle-class and working-class alike—to get rid of the outdated old fools in charge.

Trumpets around the walls of the Barbican. Trumpets turning into penny-whistles and then, reflected in the new shining glass, suddenly and surprisingly accompanied by a respectful and celebratory choir.

It is not Orwell's fault that he did not foresee the 'England, England' of advanced capitalism. But it is a fact that he popularised a version of England—all the more effective because it was a version and not a theory, a mood rather than an analysis susceptible of disproof—which in some of its very strengths and closeness has been in practice disarming.

'A foreign observer, new to England.' He was never, of course, that. But he came back from the periphery with a real and lasting hatred of imperialism and saw at the centre what his education and experience had prepared for him : 'a family with the wrong members in control'. The fact is he needed this family. He had been deprived of it, humiliated by it. Now he acted out the humiliation, trying to speak to and rally the other members of the family, trying to get them to take over.

What he could tell them about, effectively, was the imperialism they ignored, the slums they neglected. But just as it is limiting to see a capitalist system without its imperialist extension, so it is limiting to see capitalism only through imperialism and through its visible ruling class. Part of the England he discovered was a real society, living under and within this order, keeping certain values going. But inseparable from this was the different England created by this order, in prejudices, compromises, adjustments, illusions. To respond to the society would be to distinguish one part from the other, to enter a necessary conflict, reaching into every area of life. But to do that to a family, to 'England', would be unthinkable: treacherous and mean. He has lost a family and its old family pride. He is trying to join a family, to take part in a decent future. The emotions are understandable and honourable, but they are particular emotions—the emotions of the exile from a lost country, a lost class. Seen from where 'England' is happening, stretching to past and future in its more immediate and complicated processes, they are too easy, too settling, too sweet.

For 'England my England' is an assertion, a declaration of independence, a challenge. 'England your England', by contrast, is a version, a story, a dream. And when it breaks, under pressure, it will become a nightmare.

3   Being a Writer

What did it mean, in Orwell's generation, to be a writer? The question can seem naïve. Many people think that being a writer carries its own simple and self-evident definition. Yet any such definition turns out, on analysis, to have a social history; it is an idea like any other. In Orwell's case the definition is particularly important, not only as a way of understanding his achievement and his influence, but also as a way of seeing a particular kind of literary crisis, itself clearly part of a social crisis, at just the historical moment when he was learning to write.

It was the late 1920s. Seven years later Orwell wrote:

> On the last occasion when *Punch* produced a genuinely funny joke, which was only six or seven years ago, it was a picture of an intolerable youth telling his aunt that when he came down from the University he intended to 'write'. 'And what are you going to write about, dear?', his aunt enquires. 'My dear aunt', the youth replies crushingly, 'one doesn't write *about* anything, one just *writes*'. (CEJL, I, 256–7)

Orwell goes on to say that the cartoon was a 'perfectly justified criticism of current literary cant'. But this is in 1936. In fact the problem was one that he was never quite sure about, and that the state of literary argument in his period didn't help him to resolve. He was always likely, for example, even late in his life, to make a distinction of *intention* between the writing of prose and the writing of verse. This turns out, on examination, to be a distinction between writing for the effect of the content and writing for the effect of the words. In prose, though not in all prose, the former is assumed to predominate.

But this distinction itself is the product of a divided aesthetics. Language, characteristically, is taken to be an agent rather than a source of experience. Or, to put it another way, content is taken to precede language, and the writer can then choose whether to reveal content directly or to work with words for their own sake. Even if this is only a matter of emphasis rather than a rigid distinction, it is profoundly misleading. For it is always the *relation* between experience and expression, in an individual writer and in the language and forms which he shares with his society, that is really decisive.

Orwell kept coming back to this problem, as he tried to direct and understand his development. In 'Why I Write' (1946) he described his very early development, from fantasies with himself as hero to what he calls 'more and more a mere description of what I was doing and the things I saw'. That 'mere' is significant. For it is repeated in what he sees as the next stage in his adolescent development, when he suddenly discovered 'the joy of mere words, i.e., the sounds and associations of words'. Mere description, mere words. This way of seeing the literary problem remained important: not only in his development, but as one characteristic form of the underlying social crisis of his time.

What is most significant is the desire to justify himself as a writer: that problem of justification, and of seriousness, which the remembered joke had stirred into activity. He was living, after all, at a time and within a class in which the whole practice of writing was problematic. Leaving aside 'writing for entertainment'—the production of a written commodity which others would consume and, if it was pleasing, value—attitudes to writing had hardened and even polarised. In the confident middle class, intent on its version of practicality, writing was thought of as an impractical secondary activity, an alternative to 'doing something real'. Characteristically, of course, an escape route was allowed at that point where the impractical activity had practical effects: that is to say, made money. The successful author (a rather different character from the simple 'writer') was then an admired and rewarded producer, like any other. But there was not only the difficulty of stages—getting from being a writer to being a successful author. There was also the fact that on this projection the writer had no autonomous purposes: his definition of achievement would be shaped from the beginning by an external and alienated standard. At the same time a growing minority of the same social class made a related but apparently opposite abstraction in reaction to this. If the only orthodox test of achievement was 'social' recognition and success, then this could be 'opposed' by a simple negation. The 'writer', the true writer, had no commercial aims, but also, at root, no social function and, by derivation, no social content. He just 'wrote'. And then as a self-defined recognisable figure, he live 'outside' society: unconventional, the 'artist'.

This development and polarisation is a real social history. It is an important phase of nineteenth-century bourgeois life and thought, which reached its first climax in the 1880s and 1890s in most of Europe, and was still active though hardened and at times conventional in the 1920s. It has had many effects, in theory and in practice. It is at the root of the conventional distinction between 'content' and 'form' in their effective modern senses. Orwell's theoretical questions, never pushed far enough to become genuine theory, are also practical reactions to the immediate crisis of what he was to do. There are several reasons for his conscious rejection of the conventional life of his class: an attempted social identification with its victims; a search for an identity beyond its determined figures; a refusal of what it understood as success. But there is also, at least at first, a simpler reaction, into one of the prepared alternative roles. It is in this sense, I would say, that he goes to Paris, to 'be a writer': that is to say, to live 'outside' society and to 'write'. Recalling that period in 'Inside the Whale' he repeats his memory of the *Punch* joke; recalls the 'swarm of artists, writers, students, dilettanti, sight-seers, debauchees and plain idlers'; and describes its ideology: 'In "cultured" circles art-for-art's-saking extended practically to a worship of the meaningless. Literature was supposed to consist solely in the manipulation of words.' (CEJL, I, 508) Perhaps this is overstated. It is a late generalisation. But it is an interesting way of seeing the form of the literary and social crisis through which he developed.

Orwell's choice as a writer, we may now see, was in the other direction from that emphasis of the twenties. It can be said that he chose content before form, experience before words; that he became the socially conscious writer of the thirties rather than the aesthetic writer of the twenties. Certainly, to an important extent, that is how he saw it himself. But then, just as important, seeing the choice in this way he sometimes regretted it. In 'Why I Write', for example, he said that a writer has four motives: sheer egoism, aesthetic enthusiasm, historical impulse, political purpose. These sometimes contradict each other, and in degree and proportion will vary in all writers and in any writer according to his period. In a different age, he said, the first three motives would, for him, have outweighed the fourth. He would have written 'ornate or merely descriptive books'. But 'as it is I have been forced into becoming a sort of pamphleteer' (CEJL, I, 4). What is interesting there is 'forced'. He has a clear idea of himself as he might have been in a different time. He could then see his actual writing as in some ways a contradiction of his nature: 'taking your "nature" to be the state you have attained when you are first adult' (CEJL, I, 4). This is not a hypothetical nature in some quite different time. It is a 'nature' with a precise period reference, to when he was first adult, in the twenties.

What has then happened, if we accept this account, is a virtual invasion of his natural self, his natural writing, by an inevitable social and political reality. That he sees it as inevitable is of course important. How could a man, a writer, stand aside when such things were happening? But the form of this acknowledgment remains interesting. For it presupposes a situation in which a writer could choose whether to be exposed to a social and political reality. The bitterness of the thirties was that no decent man could choose not to be exposed.

But this is only a repetition in a particular form of his original and I would say persistent world-view. Men have their natures—not innate natures but their formed adult selves—which a social and political reality invades. Orwell's apparently limited statement about writing turns out, on reflection, to be a very general statement about individuals and societies. The relation between 'writing' and 'reality' is a form of the relation between men and their history.

Eric Blair, indeed, might have become somebody else:

not Orwell but X. The choice of Orwell—not the name but the actual work—was made within a very pressing general and personal history. He developed as a writer through the years of the depression and of fascism. At every point in these years he exposed himself to these facts in their most direct form. He became unemployed and penniless: partly because of the early difficulties of being a writer, but also deliberately, as a way of cutting his connections with an established and unacceptable social position. He went to Spain to fight fascism; partly, to begin with, as a way of being a writer, but then deliberately, as a way of setting his life against an evil and destructive social force. His courage and persistence in this repeated exposure to the hardest facts of his time are by any standard remarkable. Yet in and through this exposure there is an unresolved problem: that of the other self, the other writer, that he had wished and still wished to be.

The force of the desire was the whole problem. Many men, many writers, have been 'invaded'—broken in on by a history that they did not choose and that remained external to them, though disturbing and troubling. This is not, obviously, Orwell's case. The 'invasion' is actively sought, is indeed invited. And yet behind it, all the time —behind this inevitable 'content'—is another image, other words; another way of 'being a writer'.

Orwell eventually generalised this problem, in the late essay 'Writers and Leviathan':

The invasion of literature by politics was bound to happen. It must have happened, even if the special problem of totalitarianism had never arisen, because we have developed a sort of compunction which our grandparents did not have, an awareness of the enormous injustice and misery of the world, and a guilt-stricken feeling that one ought to be doing something about it, which makes a purely aesthetic attitude towards life impossible. No one, now, could devote himself to literature as single-mindedly as Joyce or Henry James. (CEJL, IV, 408–9)

This account of the invasion is significant. Totalitarianism, active interference with writers, is a special problem, but underlying it is something more general, a social conscience. And that is an invasion? Orwell usually describes his own feelings so accurately that surface analysis is hardly ever necessary; he seems to say very clearly what he means. But here he is saying that the 'social conscience' of the writer, hitherto detached but now necessarily involved, is an invasion of 'literature'. And, characteristically, his definition of literature, if only as something now unattainable, is still related to 'a purely aesthetic attitude towards life'. His example of Joyce doesn't help. Joyce wrote as he did through poverty and exile. *Finnegans Wake* was completed in 1939. That emphasis, right or wrong, was historically available. But the example of James is extremely suggestive, for it takes us back to the period when not this problem but this way of stating the problem became normal.

Reading Orwell's account quickly, one might never remember the English novelists from Dickens and Elizabeth Gaskell to George Eliot and Hardy: those contemporaries of 'our grandparents' who were indeed aware of 'the enormous injustice and misery of the world' and who in different ways made literature from just this experience. There is nothing especially new about social awareness in writers, and indeed in the nineteenth century it had been widespread and growing, especially among the novelists. But near the end of the century, and in England in relation to Henry James, an opposition between the 'social' and the 'aesthetic' was widely attempted. Not only was social experience seen as content and literature as form; also, and more dangerously, social experience was seen as only general and abstract, with the result that the definition of literary content was itself narrowed to an emphasis on abstracted 'personal relationships'. This, by the way, has little to do with James's actual work, in which social and personal experience, though certainly in a limited world, were seen as interacting and at times integral. But in his emphasis on 'handling' material, on the application of 'manner' to 'matter', James extended an understandable consciousness of technique to a point at which the wholly abstracted 'aesthetic' emphasis could seem to be reasonably made. The important quarrel between James and Wells —between a composed, pure, essentially passive art, and new kinds of projected, committed, essentially purposive writing—came at a time when the development of the novel in twentieth-century conditions was very much at issue. A deeper awareness of psychological complexities was present at the same time as a deeper awareness of social complexities. What was common was a sense of crisis, but alternative ways of describing it were in practice, each in its own way, leading to radical changes in literary form, yet each pulling in quite opposite directions.

There was, then, a real and major problem in aesthetics, in which decisions about form were inseparable from decisions about experience. But this central issue, which is still not resolved, was overlaid by a kind of capture of terms, in which 'aesthetic' and even 'literature' were associated with only one of the possible decisions. Other possible and actual decisions were described, externally, as 'anti-aesthetic' or 'sociological'. As this serious argument moved into the cant of the hangers-on, a situation was created in which even an Orwell could talk of an 'aesthetic attitude towards life' which self-evidently excluded social conscience or even social consciousness. The aesthetic attitude which mattered was of course towards art: towards its substantial, serious, and varying problems. The 'aesthetic attitude towards life' was a displaced consciousness relating to one of many possible artistic decisions but above all related to a version of society: not an artistic consciousness but a disguised social consciousness, in which the real connections and involvements with others could be plausibly overlooked and then in effect ratified: a definition of 'being a writer' which excluded social experience and social concern.

Orwell tried hard and seriously to reject the thinking of the social class in which he was educated. In a number of ways and at great personal cost he succeeded. But, ironically, the man who in practice solved some of these literary problems, in an effective and often influential way, continued to think not only that he was not solving them (a feeling natural enough to any continuing writer) but that in some way he was evading or abandoning literature: 'a sort of pamphleteering', as he said with the sneer he had been taught.

His decisions needed to be integral, for at root they were one decision. The 'aesthetic attitude towards life' was not only a way of writing novels of a particular kind. It was also, in effect, a formula, even a kind of treaty, coming at just that point in the bourgeois reduction of art which was so critical in the twentieth-century experience. We can see, looking back, how convenient it was (how convenient it often still is) to put literature into a compartment in which, to be true to itself, it should have no direct concern with social reality. This suited the people who despised literature as impractical but who in any case wanted no independent scrutiny, of any kind, of the society they were actively directing and creating. Behind the simple words of the philistine there are quite often the harder words of the controller or censor. But then the apparent opposition—the people who said they valued literature—had in practice reduced it to a safe area and, moreover, were teaching attitudes that would limit its uses to touching and tasting. No real art of whatever kind could be reduced in this way, but what mattered, in the general consciousness, was not works but attitudes—a set of emphases, omissions, encouragements, discouragements, advice, warnings. How effective this set was we can see from Orwell, regretting the development that was in fact his achievement, hating the orthodox literary world but still carrying its instructions around in his mind to nag at and weaken his creative energy.

There is another problem: Orwell's complicated responses to the modern literature he valued and his uses of some of its methods in his own work. We shall look at this in some detail in the next chapter as we trace his literary development. But something more needs to be said here about the 'invasion' by political and social reality, the forcibly altered definition of 'being a writer'. I have said that his decisions needed to be integral; that his social and political decisions—his refusal to live as an imperialist official or as the home-based equivalent— were profoundly connected with his decisions about writing. There was the failure I have noted: to get rid of the assumptions about literature that he was in practice contradicting. But there was also something else, which lay very deep in his work and which may be the fundamental reason for what was otherwise only a superficial failure.

It would be easy to say that almost all Orwell's important writing is about someone who gets away from an oppressive normality. From the central characters of *The Clergyman's Daughter* and *Keep the Aspidistra Flying* to those of *Coming Up For Air* and *Nineteen Eighty-Four*, this experience of awareness, rejection, and flight is repeatedly enacted. Yet it would be truer to say that most of Orwell's important writing is about someone who tries to get away but fails. That failure, that reabsorption, happens, in the end, in all the novels mentioned, though of course the experience of awareness, rejection, and flight has made its important mark.

The real paradox of Orwell may, then, be more clearly seen. Without the act of awareness and rejection he would not, probably, have been a writer at all. Most of his emphasis, understandably, is on that. But what if he felt, all the time, that in just this movement he was destined to fail? What if he felt, simultaneously, that the flight was necessary but also useless?

This would explain a good deal. For Orwell is then not only the man and the writer setting out on a new path, but also, could it not be, the man and the writer whose 'nature' has been invaded by an unwelcome reality, who has to live and write in these ways but who would have preferred other ways? An image of what he might have been under some other name (the renaming is crucial) is there and persists, while what he is and has chosen to be is very different. And the stress falls, necessarily, on 'chosen'. What Orwell consciously made of himself under very real pressures can be seen as an invasion of his nature: not only because of the difficulty of the choice and its break from what he has been intended to be; but also because he felt, against much of the evidence, that he would in any case fail; that he would be dragged back, reabsorbed, into the powerful orthodox world. 'Being a writer', in one definition, had been a possible way out. But being the writer he was, the real writer, led him into every kind of difficulty, every tension that the choice had seemed to offer to avoid.

4 Observation and Imagination

Orwell's writing in the thirties can be conventionally divided into the 'documentary' and 'factual' work on the one hand, and the 'fictional' and 'imaginative' work on the other. The surface distinction is evident enough: on the one hand *Down and Out in Paris and London, The Road to Wigan Pier, Homage to Catalonia*, and such sketches as 'The Spike', 'A Hanging', 'Shooting an Elephant'; on the other hand the four novels *Burmese Days, A Clergyman's Daughter, Keep the Aspidistra Flying*, and *Coming Up for Air*. Yet nothing is clearer, as we look into the work as a whole, than that this conventional division is secondary. The key problem, in all this work, is the relation between 'fact' and 'fiction': an uncertain relation which is part of the whole crisis of 'being a writer'.

Literature used not to be divided in these external ways. The rigid distinction between 'documentary' and 'imaginative' writing is a product of the nineteenth century, and most widely distributed in our own time. Its basis is a naïve definition of the 'real world', and then a naïve separation of it from the observation and imagination of men. If there is real life and its recording, on the one hand, and a separable imaginative world on the other, two kinds of literature can be confidently distinguished, and this is much more than a formal effect. In naturalist and positivist theories this effective dualism of 'the world' and 'the mind' is at least clearly recognisable. But the conventional dualism of most orthodox literary theory has scarcely been noted, let alone challenged. Terms like 'fiction' and 'non-fiction', 'documentary' and 'imaginative', continue to obscure many of the actual problems of writing.

The unity of Orwell's 'documentary' and 'imaginative' writing is the very first thing to notice. There were many problems of method, but at least Orwell got past the conventional division, if only in practice. And he saw the division as it actually presented itself to him as something more than a formal problem. He saw it, correctly, as a problem of social relationships.

> English fiction on its higher levels is for the most part written by literary gents about literary gents for literary gents; on its lower levels it is generally the most putrid 'escape' stuff—old maids' fantasies about Ian Hay male virgins, or little fat men's visions of themselves as Chicago gangsters. Books about ordinary people behaving in an ordinary manner are extremely rare, because they can only be written by someone who is capable of standing both inside and outside the ordinary man, as Joyce for instance stands inside and outside Bloom; but this involves admitting that you yourself *are* an ordinary person for nine-tenths of the time, which is exactly what no intellectual ever wants to do. (CEJL, I, 230)

There is still some unnoticed class feeling in this. Orwell is still seeing from far enough outside to suppose that there are people—a class of people—who are 'ordinary' ten-tenths of the time. But to have got as far as he did is something.

I think the interest of Bloom is that he is an ordinary

uncultivated man described from within by someone who can also stand outside him and see him from another angle. Not that Bloom is an absolutely typical man in the street. . . .

The man in the street is usually described in fiction either by writers who are themselves intellectually men in the street, tho' they may have great gifts as novelists (e.g. Trollope), or by cultivated men who describe him *from outside* (e.g. Samuel Butler, Aldous Huxley). (CEJL, I, 128)

Cultivated men who describe the man in the street from outside. It is in and through this social deformity, inflicted on him by his class and education, that Orwell reaches for the idea of an extended or even common humanity. His writing in the thirties is an exploration, in experience and in books, towards such a humanity.

The problem of social relationship is, then, a problem of form. *Down and Out in Paris and London* is in effect a journal. What is put in is the experience of being without money in a modern city: the experience of dishwashers and tramps, of filthy rooms, dosshouses, casual wards. The author is present, but only insofar as these things are happening to him along with others. His own character and motivations are sketched as briefly as those of anyone else met in the kitchen or on the road. He is neither 'inside' nor 'outside'; he is simply drifting *with* others—exceptionally close to them but within the fact that they are drifting, that this is *happening to* their bodies and minds.

But then compare *A Clergyman's Daughter*. It is a novel about a repressed girl who has a breakdown, goes vagrant, and eventually returns, via teaching, to where she started. Anyone who reads Orwell's other writing of the time will find most of the experiences of the novel elsewhere in other forms. The 'Church Times' and the glue-and-brown-paper theatrical armour, and even the 'moribund hag who stinks of mothballs and gin, and has to be more or less carried to and from the altar' are to be found in Chapter One of the novel and in Orwell's letters about himself (CEJL, I, 103, 105, 101–2). Or the girl going vagrant, the hop-picking, Ginger and Deafie, sleeping rough in Trafalgar Square: these are to be found in Chapter Two and the beginning of Chapter Three, also in Orwell's diary, 'Hop-Picking' (CEJL, I, 52–71). The point is not the external relation between the writer's 'material' and his 'process of creation'. The interest is almost entirely in the method of handling the author's own presence: the intermediary character of the girl— 'inside' when she is caught in the routines of church and teaching; 'outside', even amnesiac, when she is drifting on the road. The attempted characterisation of the girl as more than a surrogate presence is at times serious and detailed, at times merely functional. But a *sustained* identity, through diversity and dislocation of experience, cannot yet be realised. And it is interesting that at one point—the night scene in Trafalgar Square, in the first section of Chapter Three—Orwell makes a conscious literary experiment of a different, impersonal kind, which is very evidently derived from the night-town chapter in *Ulysses*—the novel that had been so much in his mind as an example. He remained pleased with this experiment, though coming to reject the book as a whole.

Orwell's affinity to Joyce—or attempted affinity—is not in our usual reading. The modern writers Orwell mentions most often, in his earlier period, are Wells,

Bennett, Conrad, Hardy, Kipling. In 1940 he makes a different list—Joyce, Eliot, and Lawrence. This change of emphasis through the 1930s is quite normal and representative. Among earlier writers on his 1940 list, he names Shakespeare, Swift, Fielding, Dickens, Reade, Butler, Zola, and Flaubert. The critical interest in Shakespeare, Swift, and Dickens can be seen from his essays. But in the development of his own writing there are two opposite emphases: the detailed interest in *Ulysses* (notably in a letter to Brenda Salkeld, CEJL, I, 125–9) at just the time of working on *A Clergyman's Daughter*, and also, as he said in 1940, 'I believe the modern writer who has influenced me most is Somerset Maugham, whom I admire immensely for his power of telling a story straightforwardly and without frills' (CEJL, II, 24).

The names as such do not greatly matter. Literary influence is a secondary business. What is important is the problem of standpoint, which is the key to any critical judgment of Orwell. It is easy to say that *Down and Out in Paris and London* is better than *A Clergyman's Daughter*, but this ought not to be reduced to the plausible generalisation that he is a better 'observer' than 'novelist'. The real problem lies deeper, in the available conceptions of 'the novel'.

'Telling a story straightforwardly and without frills.' 'Story', after all, is the whole question. Maugham is the characteristic Edwardian 'storyteller' : that is to say, the collector and retailer of human episodes. Orwell had the material for this (it is usually collected at a distance, and in other lands), but only his first novel, *Burmese Days*, is at all of its kind. Even there, while the plot concerns personal intrigue among an isolated European group on an Eastern station, the stress is on the complicated social consequences of imperialism and within this there is what we can now recognise as the deep Orwell pattern: the man who tries to break from the standards of his group but who is drawn back into it and, in this case, destroyed. What is unique about the novel in Orwell's work is that he creates an entire social and physical milieu within which the social criticism and the personal break are defined elements. In all his later novels, the essential form is shaped by what became separated elements: the personal break, and social criticism through it, in the novels of the thirties; the social criticism, with the personal break inside it, in *Nineteen Eighty-Four*.

That seems a clear development, but what it omits is the material of 'observation'. Having found one form for this, in the journal of *Down and Out in Paris and London*, Orwell clearly wanted to incorporate it in a novel. This is the developmental significance of *A Clergyman's Daughter*, where the direct observation and the fiction are unusually close. But from then on he seems to have accepted the division between 'documentary' and 'fiction'. A possible reshaping of the novel was evaded, or proved too difficult: not, I would say, because he was 'not really a novelist' but because a problem of consciousness, which he shared with other writers of his time, emerged as a problem of form.

For Orwell the interest of Joyce had been his direct realisation of 'ordinary' experience. It is Bloom he selects from *Ulysses*: that recording 'inside' and 'outside' the ordinary man. But this description conceals the problem of the relationship of the novelist to his character, which is always a form of relationship of the writer to his world. And the relationship that matters here can be alternatively described as 'acceptance' or 'passivity'. It is an impersonal form, the logical consequence of James's emphasis on the artist's 'handling' of 'matter'. It is 'the artist refined out of existence', observing, recording. Except that in practice it is impossible to observe anything without being in some relationship to it. The apparent relationship, that which is recommended and publicised, is the 'aesthetic'; the 'handling' of the matter, the preoccupation with words, that is Joyce's actual development. But the 'matter' can only be handled in this way—can only be abstracted, stay still to be 'written'—if a particular relationship is in fact assumed. 'Acceptance' or 'passivity': the difference between the positive and negative descriptions is less important than the fact of the relationship itself—a refraining from intervention, or, more, a seeing no need to intervene, since the availability of the 'matter' is the artist's primary and only concern.

Orwell's artistic failure, in his novels of the thirties, is in a way and paradoxically due to his social achievement. He had known passivity at least, very closely, as he describes in *Down and Out in Paris and London*. But he had known it not in his capacity as a writer but as its victim, and insofar as it was 'matter' it was matter of a kind that concerned him personally rather than as a writer. What we have seen him describe as an 'invasion' is the growth of that social consciousness which required his intervention, which made either acceptance or passivity impossible (though he went back to the idea of acceptance and passivity, in *Inside the Whale*, at a time when the social intervention could be held to have failed).

And then in shaping a literary form, he created the figure of the intermediary (the 'shock-absorber of the bourgeoisie' as he once referred to people like himself). Instead of direct realisation of what was observed, he created the intermediary figure who goes around and to whom things happen. This figure, in the novels, is not himself, and this is very important. The figure has his experiences, in *A Clergyman's Daughter* and then in a different way in *Keep the Aspidistra Flying*. The figure is passive; things happen *to* Dorothy, or *to* Comstock. And this pattern releases one element of Orwell's experience —the things that had 'happened' to him—but not or only partly why they had happened, not the intervening or 'invading' consciousness. Dorothy, certainly, is the more passive figure. Comstock, in *Keep the Aspidistra Flying*, is given some of Orwell's whole consciousness: not only trying to live without money but declaring war on money and its system. Comstock is an active and critical figure in all the initial exploration, but increasingly there is a contradiction within the mode of observation. The active and resourceful persistence of Orwell, the impressive survival and remaking of an active self, is steadily cut out, as the accepting observation continues. What begins as a protest becomes a whine, and the reabsorption of Comstock into a world of manipulable objects is accomplished with a kind of perverse triumph: the 'character' of the intermediary (like the 'character' of Flory or of Dorothy) being the 'justification' of the eventual submission or defeat.

This is the strange transmutation of 'acceptance' or 'passivity'. In Orwell, because of his uncertainties, it is neither an artistic discipline nor an acceptable worldview. His final attempt at a Bloom figure is Bowling in *Coming Up For Air*, written at a recollecting and abstracting distance and perhaps for that reason more consistent internally. Bowling breaks from an orthodox routine, like the others, though not into exposure, where things happen to him; but instead into the past, an old England and his childhood; and then the experience is of loss, disillusion, disenchantment. *Coming Up For Air* came after Orwell's crucial political experience in Spain and its consequences, which we shall have to look at in detail. But elements of the literary decision are continuous: observation through a limited intermediary, with the limit as the basis for a deeper pattern: a self-proving of both the need and the impossibility of a sustained break, so that active intervention dwindles to a temporary protest or self-assertion. The significance of this pattern in the altered world of *Nineteen Eighty-Four* will need further analysis, when the other changes have been taken into account.

Having failed to solve his profoundly difficult problem in the novel, Orwell turned to other forms which were in practice more available. His social and political writing was a direct release of consciousness, the practical consequence of intervention. 'Shooting an Elephant', for example, is more successful than anything in *Burmese Days* not because it is 'documentary' rather than fiction—the fiction, as we have seen, similarly relied on things that had happened to him—but because instead of a Flory an Orwell is present: a successfully created character in every real sense. Instead of diluting his consciousness through an intermediary, as the mode of fiction had seemed to require, he now writes directly and powerfully about his whole experience. The prose is at once strengthened, as the alternation between an anxious impersonation and a passively impersonal observation gives way to a direct voice, in which there is more literary creation than in all the more conventionally 'imaginative' attempts.

'Shooting an Elephant' is not a document; it is a literary work. The distinction between 'fiction' and 'non-fiction' is not a matter of whether the experience happened to the writer, a distinction between 'real' and 'imaginary'. The distinction that matters is always one of range and consciousness. Written human experience of an unspecialised and primary kind must always be recognised as literature. Particular forms, and the origins of the material, are secondary questions. Orwell began to write literature, in the full sense, when he found this 'non-fictional' form : that is, when he found a form capable of realising his experience directly.

Realising *his* experience—not only what had happened to him and what he had observed, but what he felt about it and what he thought about it, the self-definition of 'Orwell', the man inside and outside the experience. Perhaps the best example is *The Road to Wigan Pier*. As it happens Orwell's diary notes for this book have been published (CEJL, I, 170–214). A comparison of the diary and the book is interesting, for a number of reasons. It is easy enough to find in the notes the sources of many of the descriptions : of the Brookers' lodging house, for example, in the opening chapter. But what is also evident, comparing the two, is the literary process. There is the expected and necessary development of a scene, in the published version : a fuller and more fluent description, details recollected from memory. But there is also a saturation of the scene with feeling. Orwell is present and responding, indeed directing response, in a way that is only there towards the end in the diary notes. He seems also to have shifted the lodgers around a bit : Joe, at the Brookers', is described in the notes as a lodger at a previous house—a house which is not in the book. So in the book the Brookers' house is not only given the emphasis of the first place but treated as a first, representative experience ('it struck me that this place must be fairly normal as lodging-houses in the industrial areas go') when in the diary there is a preceding and rather different experience.

This is just one small example to illustrate the point about 'documentary' experience. The writer shapes and organises what happened to produce a particular effect, based on experience but then created out of it. The overall organisation of *The Road to Wigan Pier* is a major example. In the first part, the 'observation' of the industrial north, one of the key points, in literary terms, is that Orwell is the isolated observer going around and seeing for himself. This created character is then used to important effect in the second half, the argument about socialism, where the man who has gone and seen for himself is contrasted with the jargon-ridden bourgeois socialists: 'The first thing that must strike any outside observer is that Socialism in its developed form is a theory confined entirely to the middle class' (RWP, 173).

The external political point is not what is most important here: 'in its developed form' is an infinitely saving clause. The key point is the persona, the 'outside observer'—that is, Orwell. An essential link between the two parts is indeed this character: 'inside' and then 'outside' the experience.

We learn from the diary notes that after some days wandering on his own through the Midlands Orwell was given some political contacts in Lancashire and met working-class socialists and members of the Unemployed Workers' Movement. Through one of these contacts he got the chance to go down a mine; and through the NUWM collectors he obtained facts about housing conditions. It is important that he omits most of this experience—an actual social and political network—in *The Road to Wigan Pier*. Even in the diary, some of the difficulties are apparent. A local trade union official and his wife, 'both ... working-class people', are seen as living (in a twelve or fourteen-shilling-a-week estate house) in an 'entirely middle-class' atmosphere (CEJL, I, 173). Orwell has his own definition of what the working class is like. That is, presumably, why he could say, after meeting these people (who had embarrassed him by calling him 'comrade') and 'an electrician who takes a prominent part in the Socialist movement', that 'socialism' was a middle-class affair. If a working man is a socialist he is already, presumably, middle-class, the character of the working-class being already known.

But here the political point *is* the literary point. What is created in the book is an isolated independent observer and the objects of his observation. Intermediate characters and experiences which do not form part of this world—this structure of feeling—are simply omitted. What is left in is 'documentary' enough, but the process of selection and organisation is a literary act: the character of the observer is as real and yet created as the real and yet created world he so powerfully describes.

All of Orwell's writing until 1937 is, then, a series of works and experiments around a common problem. Instead of dividing them into 'fiction' and 'documentaries' we should see them as sketches towards the creation of his most successful character, 'Orwell'. It would not be so successful if it had not been so intensely and painfully lived. The exposure to poverty and suffering and filth and waste was as real as it was deliberate, and the record of the exposure is a remarkable enlargement of our literature. But in and through the exposure a character is being created, who is real in the precise sense that he becomes this writer, this shaping presence. Flory and Dorothy and Comstock, or the later Bowling, are aspects of this character but without its centrality. The only literary form which can contain the full character at this stage is the 'non-fiction journal' of an isolated writer exposed to a suffering but unconnecting world. The need to intervene, to force active connections, is the road away from Wigan Pier, back to an indifferent and sleepy and uncaring world, which has to be told about the isolation and the suffering.

At just this point, between the diary and the book, the Spanish war broke out. The writing, and the character, moved into a different dimension.

5 Politics

Orwell's original intention in going to Spain was to 'gather materials for newspaper articles etc.' (CEJL, I, 316). But he was told that to get into Spain he needed papers from some organisation of the Left. Victor Gollancz had started the Left Book Club in May 1936; its selection committee consisted of Gollancz, Harold Laski, and John Strachey. *The Road to Wigan Pier* was to be published in March 1937 by the Left Book Club, though with a cautionary note. It was through Strachey that Orwell made his first attempt to get papers for Spain, going with an introduction to Harry Pollitt of the Communist Party, who asked if he would undertake to join the International Brigade. Orwell replied that he could not undertake to join anything until he had seen what was happening. He then made contact with the Independent Labour Party, with whom previously he had 'some slight connection', and was given a letter of introduction to John McNair in Barcelona. It was mainly because of this letter that when he decided to fight he joined the militia of the POUM, with which the ILP had connections. As it happened, joining the POUM militia pushed him into the centre of an intricate and bitter political struggle between rival socialist groups. But as we can see from the way things went, and in particular from his original approach through Strachey to Pollitt, this was in no way of his own seeking. He had been critical of what he knew as Marxist theory, of its jargon and its sectarian and factional feuds, before he left England. As he argued in *The Road to Wigan Pier*, the urgent duty of socialists—to make more people act like socialists—was being hindered by what seemed to him an alienated atmosphere and style. He thought of himself as an anti-imperialist and an anti-fascist, as a believer in equality, and only through these positions as a socialist. Joining the militia of the POUM was not an affiliation in the conventional political sense. What he had criticised among socialists and Marxists in Britain he found in the POUM as much as in the Communist Party in Spain. But it was the readiest way in which he could fight against the fascists, and at first the doctrinal differences hardly mattered to him. Some months later, when he knew much more about them, he took the same attitude when he wanted to go to fight in Madrid, asking for a recommendation from a friend in the Communist Party. For still, as he said, fighting where he could be most useful was his primary concern; the shades of political doctrine were at best secondary. Indeed, 'as far as my purely personal preferences went I would have liked to join the Anarchists', but serving on the most critical front came first.

These details are important, both for the record (which has become very confused) and for the clear impression they give of Orwell's undoctrinal socialism. It can indeed be argued that socialism as such was always secondary, in his mind, to the struggle against fascism and imperialism and inequality. Socialism was a general idea, a general name, against all these evils, and before he left England it had little more positive content. The experience of revolutionary Barcelona determined him to fight, rather than any positive affiliation conceived in Britain. It was the first time he had ever been 'in a town where the working class was in the saddle' (HC, 8). His 'vague idea of fighting if it seemed worthwhile' was transformed by this new experience, and joining the militia to fight the fascists 'seemed the only conceivable thing to do'. In the militia 'many of the normal motives of civilized life—snobbishness, money-grubbing, fear of the boss, etc.—had simply ceased to exist. The ordinary class-division of society had disappeared to an extent that is almost unthinkable in the money-tainted air of England' (HC, 102).

The experience was, in a true sense, a political breakthrough:

> One had been in a community where hope was more normal than apathy or cynicism, where the word 'comrade' stood for comradeship and not, as in most countries, for humbug ... In that community where no one was on the make, where there was a shortage of everything but no privilege and no boot-licking, one got, perhaps, a crude forecast of what the opening stages of Socialism might be like. And, after all, instead of disillusioning me it deeply attracted me. The effect was to make my desire to see Socialism established much more actual than it had been before. (HC, 102–3)

Or, as he put it even more strongly in a letter of June 1937, when he was preparing to leave Spain, 'I have seen wonderful things and at last really believe in Socialism, which I never did before' (CEJL, I, 269).

This emphasis is crucial. During those months in Spain Orwell became a revolutionary socialist. Up to a point there is a clear line from his experience in the years of poverty, exposure, and rejection of privilege—the wandering years—to the experience of shared hardship in Barcelona. But there is also a clear break, from a personal option to a common cause. What had been mainly a passive exposure to the worst kinds of hardship became an active involvement in the struggle to end them. It is, then, ironic that at the moment when Orwell became a revolutionary socialist he became involved with an internal struggle so deep and lasting that it is still very difficult to see his experience and his development clearly.

While he was at the front in the early months of 1937 he listened to endless arguments about the future of the war and the revolution. The situation was indeed so complicated that there was virtually no limit to argument. In broad outline, it was said on the one hand that everything must be subordinated to the duty of defeating the fascist armies, and on the other hand that fascism could be defeated only if there was a simultaneous social revolution. In subsequent historical accounts, these cases have been repeated and examined, in great detail and often with bitterness. To move in that area at all is like moving in a minefield. Most historians have taken the view that the revolution—mainly anarcho-syndicalist but with the POUM taking part—was an irrelevant distraction from a desperate war. Some, at the time and after, have gone so far as to describe it as deliberate sabotage of the war effort. Only a few have argued on the other side, that the suppression of the revolution by the main body of Republican forces was an act of power politics, related to Soviet policy, which amounted to a betrayal of the cause for which the Spanish people were fighting.

As we have seen, the experience of revolutionary Barcelona made Orwell a militant socialist. But in the chaos and inactivity of the early months at the front, he usually supported the Communist line. It seemed to him a matter of practical common sense that there should be unity and efficiency; indeed, echoes of his own early training as an officer cadet and in the Imperial Police can be heard again and again as he describes the disorganisation of the revolutionary militia. At the same time, his experience of its revolutionary spirit, its practical comradeship, was paramount. This, before everything, was why he was fighting at all.

It is difficult to say how this conflict would have resolved itself if the situation had not changed. The contrary impulses in Orwell's mind were only too clearly reflected in the immediate pressures. From his education and training he believed in efficiency as an isolated value. From his social development during the wandering years in England he had come to believe, profoundly, in the common cause of the oppressed, and was impatient of political divisions which delayed or prevented its expression. In both these respects he was a natural Popular Front man, and the official Republican argument impressed him. But his previously passive belief in a common cause had been realised and released by the revolutionary experience: the sense of living in a new human world. When he went back to Barcelona after three and a half months at the front, he found a different city. In December 1936 it had been a place 'where class distinctions and great differences of wealth hardly existed'. Now 'things were returning to normal. The smart restaurants and hotels were full of rich people wolfing expensive meals, while for the working-class population food-prices had jumped enormously without any corresponding rise in wages' (HC, 110). The revolutionary atmosphere was disappearing, in almost every respect, and the working class no longer even seemed to be in control. This was not only the result of political changes, leading to the end of the popular militia and the reorganisation of a centralised army and administration. But when the power struggle, implicit in these changes, erupted in what looked now like a 'normal' city, Orwell's sympathies would not have been in doubt, quite apart from the fact that having served in the POUM militia he was part of the movement that was declared illegal and suppressed. His account of that fighting brings out its extraordinary complexity, and he is quick to say that he can only report what he saw and that like every other account his own is partisan and subject to bias and error. But what happened to him and his comrades from the front was so arbitrary and brutal that his choice of action was inevitable. Different accounts were given, and are still given, of the start of the street-fighting and of its political motives. All Orwell knew, and could know, was that the ragged men back from the front, in this again class-divided city, were being rounded up by guards and police in the name of the struggle against fascism, and, most accounts say, in the name of the true cause of socialism and of the people. The experience left a scar which was never likely to heal. One would think worse of him, indeed, if it had ever healed.

Homage to Catalonia is in some ways Orwell's most important and most moving book. It is an unforgettably vivid personal account of a revolution and a civil war. But it has been less highly valued than some of his earlier and later writing for political reasons of a double kind. His inevitably controversial accounts of the internal struggles have cut the book off, then and since, from many readers on the Left. But also, and less often noted, his open and moving commitment to revolutionary socialism has cut the book off from a different and much larger group of readers, who from his later work have a fixed idea of Orwell as the voice of political disillusion, of the inevitable failure of revolution and of socialism. There is material for this view in *Homage to Catalonia*, in the account of the loss and suppression of the revolutionary spirit—'it was simply a temporary and local phase in an enormous game that is being played over the whole surface of the earth' (HC, 102).

Yet in none of his writing about Spain does Orwell draw what can later be seen as the right-wing conclusion. Though the revolutionary movement to which he belonged had been suppressed, he returned from Spain a convinced revolutionary socialist: 'when I see an actual flesh-and-blood worker in conflict with his natural enemy, the policeman, I do not have to ask myself which side I am on' (HC, 119). He was certainly suspicious, as he had been before he went, of what he called 'bourgeois communism', with its idealised 'worker'. But in the actual conflict he had made his choice. He was very bitter about official communist policy in Spain, and about the foreign reporting of the Spanish struggle. This hatred of what he was already calling 'Stalinism' never left him. But his position after the Spanish experience is that of a revolutionary socialist: what would now, from the outside, be called an 'ultra'. His account of the Spanish struggle is very similar to later accounts of the struggles in Budapest or in Paris: written from a revolutionary socialist position and bitterly hostile at once to the capitalist order and to orthodox communism. This stage of Orwell's political development needs exceptional emphasis.

It is perhaps of even more interest to see how and when Orwell moved from this position to the position of his last years. For example, when he wrote 'Looking Back on the Spanish War' in 1942 and long after his controversies with what he saw as the official lying of the Communist press, it was still fascism that he saw as the totalitarian danger. It was fascist propaganda, and such pro-Franco propaganda as that of the *Daily Mail* and the *Catholic Herald*, which led him to reflect that 'the very concept of objective truth is fading out of the world' (CEJL, II, 258). And it was from Nazi theory that he drew the concept of 'a nightmare world in which the Leader, or some ruling clique, controls not only the future but *the past*. If the Leader says of such and such an event, "It never happened"—well, it never happened. If he says that two and two are five—well, two and two are five' (CEJL, II, 259). These direct anticipations of *Nineteen Eighty-Four* are primarily responses to fascism, and the 're-institution of slavery', which he also sees happening, is based on the Nazi labour-camps. Nothing could be more false than the quite general idea that Orwell returned from Spain a disillusioned social-ist, who then gave his energy to warnings against a totalitarian socialist future.

Yet tracing the real development is undoubtedly diffi-cult. In 1938 Orwell joined the Independent Labour Party and explained, 'One has got to be actively a Social-ist, not merely sympathetic to Socialism, or one plays into the hands of our always-active enemies' (CEJL, I, 337–8). He said that 'for perhaps ten years past' he had had 'some grasp of the real nature of capitalist society' and that while he hoped the Labour Party would win the next election, he had no illusions about its socialism and did not intend to be 'led up the garden path in the name of capitalist democracy'.

Again in 1938, he defended the anti-war movement against the implication that pacifism was a soft option for intellectuals.

The truth is that any real advance, let alone any genuinely revolutionary change, can only begin when the mass of the people definitely refuse capitalist–imperialist war ... So long as they show themselves willing to fight 'in defence of democracy', or 'against Fascism', or for any other flyblown slogan, the same trick will be played upon them again and again. (CEJL, I, 331)

Reviewing Borkenau's *The Communist International* he wrote:

If the problems of western capitalism are to be solved, it will have to be through a third alternative, a movement which is genuinely revolutionary, i.e. willing to make drastic changes and to use violence if necessary, but which does not lose touch, as Communism and Fascism have done, with the essential values of democracy. Such a thing is by no means unthinkable. The germs of such a movement exist in numerous countries, and they are capable of growing. (CEJL, I, 350)

In January 1939 he wrote to Herbert Read:

I believe it is vitally necessary for those of us who intend to oppose the coming war to start organising for illegal anti-war activities ... I quite agree that people, especially people who have any kind of notoriety, can get the best results by fighting in the open, but we might find it extremely useful to have an underground organisation *as well*. (CEJL, I, 377–8)

In this and a further letter to Read he made practical suggestions for underground activity, in a political situation in which most of the Left would have compromised and in which the 'dissident lefts like ourselves' would be the only alternative opposition to the fascists. In July 1939, writing about British Imperialism, he asked: 'What meaning would there be, even if it were successful, in bringing down Hitler's system in order to stabilise something that is far bigger and in its different way just as bad?' (CEJL, I, 397).

It is worth adding that during this period of revolutionary anti-war socialism, Orwell was not, in the jargon he so frequently criticised, a 'Trotskyite'. He often argued that this description was simply loose abuse, though he used 'Stalinist' himself. But in just this period he made it clear that he believed the faults of the Soviet Union went back to 'the aims and nature of the Bolshevik Party': 'Trotsky, in exile, denounces the Russian dictatorship, but he is probably as much responsible for it as any man now living' (CEJL, I, 381).

Attempting a new definition of revolutionary socialism, Orwell found no effective organisational home, though he continued to hope and plan for one.

Then came the change: almost overnight, as it seems. It was not simply a reaction to the beginning of the war, or even to the Stalin–Hitler agreement. Indeed

the night before the Russo–German pact was announced I dreamed that the war had started. It was one of those dreams which, whatever Freudian inner meaning they may have, do sometimes reveal to you the real state of your feelings. It taught me two things, first, that I should be simply relieved when the long-dreaded war started, secondly, that I was patriotic at heart, would not sabotage or act against my own side, would support the war, would fight in it if possible. (CEJL, I, 539)

He had been back in England since late March. His father had died in June. In the essay from which the account of the dream comes, 'My Country Right or Left', he spoke of growing up just too young for the 1914–18 war, and 'you felt yourself a little less than a man, because you had missed it'. He had had frequent military training, since childhood and the cadet corps, and 'part of the fascination that the Spanish civil war had for people of about my age was that it was so like the Great War'. Reviewing Muggeridge's *The Thirties* in the following spring, he wrote:

> It is the emotion of the middle-class man, brought up in the military tradition, who finds in the moment of crisis that he is a patriot after all. It is all very well to be 'advanced' or 'enlightened', to snigger at Colonel Blimp and proclaim your emancipation from all traditional loyalties, but a time comes when the sand of the desert is sodden red and what have I done for thee, England, my England? As I was brought up in this tradition myself I can recognise it under strange disguises, and also sympathise with it, for even at its stupidest and most sentimental it is a comelier thing than the shallow self-righteousness of the left-wing intelligentsia. (CEJL, I, 535)

On this explanation, Orwell's abrupt change is simply a reversion to type. And in a sense this is true. But under the simple readjustment, which was traditionally available, a more profound process of discouragement had been occurring. This is (following *Coming Up for Air*) directly indicated in 'Inside the Whale', written during the summer of 1939, when in relation to Henry Miller he writes sympathetically of passivity:

the viewpoint of a man who believes the world-process to be outside his control and who in any case hardly wishes to control it ... Progress and reaction have both turned out to be swindles. Seemingly there is nothing left but quietism—robbing reality of its terrors by simply submitting to it. Get inside the whale—or rather, admit that you are inside the whale (for you *are*, of course). Give yourself over to the world-process, stop fighting against it or pretending that you control it; simply accept it, endure it, record it. (CEJL, I, 519, 526)

This is his prescription for a writer, under the dangers of his time, but in a more general way it marks his real discouragement. He had exposed himself to so much hardship and then fought so hard; had got a bullet in the throat in Spain; had been severely ill with a tubercular lesion; had given so much of his energy to what seemed a desert of political illusions, lies, and bad faith. Between the myth of 'England' and this profound European disillusion he had to make what settlements he could find.

This is the right way, I think, to follow his subsequent political development. Much of Orwell's wartime journalism is lively but it is not his best work. In his criticism of people who went on holding or who came to hold positions identical or close to his own between 1937 and 1939, there is some lively polemic but also a good deal of rancour and even random abuse. Under the desperate pressures of the time, as he had reason to know as well as anyone, it was hardly possible to find any decent and consistent position, and the sectarian squabbling, the branding and naming of 'defeatist' groups, had a smallness and meanness which at times he recognised. In his diary of 27 April 1942 he noted, 'We are all drowning in filth. When I talk to anyone or read the writings of anyone who has any axe to grind, I feel that intellectual honesty and balanced judgment have simply disappeared from the face of the earth. Everyone's thought is forensic . . .' (CEJL, II, 423). And this is as true, it seems to me, of his own wartime articles as of those he criticised—but not wholly true. There is hysterical overstatement in the very face of overstatement and hysteria. At a public level, apart from his attacks on 'defeatists', and apart from his work at the BBC—where he very genuinely tried to keep the propaganda to India 'decent'—he attempted for some time to combine support for the war with a programme of turning it into a revolutionary war: defeating Hitler and the English class system simultaneously. It was a hope like any other, but the characteristic Orwell note returns when in late 1944 he publicly reviewed all the errors of analysis he had made through these years and concluded: 'whether we "opposed" the war or whether we "supported" it, I think the first admission we ought to make is that *we were all wrong*' (CEJL, III, 294). It is at one level a reasonable admission, characteristic of Orwell's profound honesty and frankness. But at another level it introduces an element which was to combine with the more submerged despairs: the notion that all political thinking, or almost all, was a mode of adjustment to one's own wishes and fantasies. As he wrote in 1946:

It is not easy to believe in the survival of civilisation . . . I think one must continue the political struggle, just as a doctor must try to save the life of a patient who is probably going to die. But . . . we shall get nowhere unless we start by recognising that political behaviour is largely non-rational, that the world is suffering from some kind of mental disease which must be diagnosed before it can be cured. (CEJL, IV, 248–9)

This is the conclusion that matters, in understanding his last work. Certainly it was given a political superstructure, the key element of which was the substitution of communism for fascism as the totalitarian threat. This was part of the movement of the times, in the early years of the cold war. But given Orwell's experience and development, it was crucial. He saw the atomic bomb as a major turning-point: 'Either we renounce it or it destroys us' (November 1945: CEJL, IV, 19). But the political shapes were altering. In 1943 he had written:

The dreary world which the American millionaires and their British hangers-on intend to impose upon us begins to take shape. The British people, in the mass, don't want such a world... Sentimentally, the majority of people in this country would rather be in a tie-up with Russia than with America. (CEJL, II, 282)

By late 1947 this was reversed:

'If you *had* to choose between Russia and America, which would you choose?' ... We are no longer strong enough to stand alone, and if we fail to bring a western European union into being, we shall be obliged, in the long run, to subordinate our policy to that of one Great Power or the other. And in spite of all the fashionable chatter of the moment, everyone knows in his heart that we should choose America. (CEJL, IV, 398)

Beneath these political adjustments was the deeper fear that the world would fall apart into two or three super-states, each holding the atomic bomb, and that within each such state there would be a new authoritarianism: what he came to call, in a phrase taken from Borkenau, 'oligarchical collectivism'. This is, of course, the world of *Nineteen Eighty-Four*, but it is significant that in just these critical years Orwell diagnosed a future based on power politics, the permanent war economy and authoritarianism—trends which he saw everywhere, behind almost all the political labels—and then identified it, directly, only with the Soviet system. He remained a democratic socialist. He gave most of his political energies to the defence of civil liberties over a wide front. But in his deepest vision of what was to come, he had at once actualised a general nightmare and then, in the political currents of the time, narrowed its reference until the nightmare itself became one of its own shaping elements.

6   Projections

Orwell began writing *Animal Farm* in November 1943. It was completed three months later. Several publishers rejected it, some on political grounds. It is ironic that a book written against the grain of prevailing public opinion should have appeared, eighteen months later, at a time when the political situation had changed and it could be used, eagerly, in what was becoming the cold war.

For a long time the book was inseparable from that ironic political context. Orwell was described on the Left as having run 'shrieking into the arms of the capitalist publishers' (*Marxist Quarterly*, January 1956), which was certainly not how it felt to him at the time ('I am having hell and all to find a publisher for it here though normally I have no difficulty in publishing my stuff'). At the same time, the book was undoubtedly used by people with whom Orwell had no sympathy and when followed by *Nineteen Eighty-Four*, which was even more extensively used, it fixed a version of Orwell which he, at least, would have considered misleading. The whole story of the refusal and then the promotion of *Animal Farm* is full of ironies of the kind Orwell was now directly concerned with, including the episode of the special edition for Ukrainian refugees of which nearly half was seized by the American authorities in Germany and handed over to Soviet officials (CEJL, IV, 379).

Animal Farm is unique in Orwell's writing in the absence of an Orwell figure. It is in this sense a more complete projection of his way of seeing the world than anything else he wrote. Yet the terms of the projection limited the consciousness with which the Orwell figure had been invented to deal. It is a work of simplification, in both the good and bad senses.

Orwell described it once as a squib (CEJL, III, 95) but it was always more serious than that. He wrote in the preface to the Ukrainian edition:

> Nothing has contributed so much to the corruption of the original idea of Socialism as the belief that Russia is a Socialist country and that every act of its rulers must be excused, if not imitated. And so for the past ten years I have been convinced that the destruction of the Soviet myth was essential if we wanted a revival of the Socialist movement. On my return from Spain I thought of exposing the Soviet myth in a story that could be easily understood by almost anyone and which could be easily translated into other languages. (CEJL, III, 405)

The precision of his political aim, and yet the search for simplicity and generality, carry some inevitable contradictions. More important, perhaps, is Orwell's emphasis on the destruction of the myth of Soviet Society, which he believed was common among the Left in the West. Perhaps that intention, at some stage, was paramount. For in the same preface he goes so far as to say:

> Even if I had the power, I would not wish to interfere in Soviet domestic affairs; I would not condemn Stalin and his associates merely for their barbaric and undemocratic methods. It is quite possible that, even with the best intentions, they could not have acted other-

wise under the conditions prevailing there. (CEJL, III, 404)

But not only did no recognition of that kind appear in the work itself; it could not have appeared, given its stress on actual conditions and on a particular historical situation, in any work conceived and executed as a general fable. Indeed, by the time the specific situation had been so generally translated, it was always possible, even likely, that not only the myth of Soviet socialism, but also the myth of revolution, would in fact be 'destroyed'.

Certainly *Animal Farm* has been widely interpreted in this way. Orwell is produced as 'evidence' against a new revolutionary generation. The revival of the Socialist movement, which he said he wanted, is met by the sad ghost of his late imagination. Perhaps this was inevitable in the exploitation of literature by the politics of the cold war. But something deeper has to be faced: the real consciousness of the fable itself. Past the easy exploitation and the equally easy rejection, the fable in *Animal Farm* offers positive and negative evidence of a permanently interesting kind.

Orwell got the germ of the fable from seeing

a little boy, perhaps ten years old, driving a huge cart-horse along a narrow path, whipping it whenever it tried to turn. It struck me that if only such animals became aware of their strength we should have no power over them, and that men exploit animals in much the same way as the rich exploit the proletariat. (CEJL, III, 406)

This insight is already of a rather different kind from the eventual projection. The speed of his figurative transition from animals to the proletariat is interesting—showing as it does a residue of thinking of the poor as animals: powerful but stupid. Men, of course, here and in the story, are seen as exploiters. And the worst thing about the Bolshevik pigs, in the story, is that they become indistinguishable from drunken, greedy, and cruel men. The noble beast is the workhorse, Boxer.

It is worth considering this alongside Orwell's remarks on Swift's Houyhnhnms and Yahoos (CEJL, IV, 217–19). He is quick to diagnose Swift's disgust with men and apparent preference for animals, but he goes on to say that actually the Houyhnhnms, whom he finds unattractive, are more like men than the Yahoos, who are a deliberate degradation. Very complicated feelings are involved here. The powerful but stupid horses of *Animal Farm* are looked on with great respect and pity. The men and the pigs are intelligent, calculating, greedy, and cruel. This is surely more than a simple operative analogy. It is a substantial, even physical response.

The other element of the analogy is exploitation. If *they* became aware of their strength, *we* should have no power over them. Orwell here is thinking about something more than a political event, about a range of relations in man's use of animals and of nature. The point he goes on to is in any other terms very surprising:

I proceeded to analyse Marx's theory from the animals' point of view. To them it was clear that the concept of a class struggle between humans was pure illusion, since whenever it was necessary to exploit animals, all humans united against them: the true struggle is between animals and humans. From this point of departure, it was not difficult to elaborate the story. (CEJL, III, 406)

The true struggle between animals and humans: is that the real theme of *Animal Farm*? It is difficult to say so, without most of the surface of the story collapsing. What really happens, I think, is that the very deep identification between the labouring and exploited animals and the labouring and exploited poor is retained, almost unnoticed, as a base for the exposure of that 'pure illusion ... of a class struggle between humans'— humans, now, being capitalists and revolutionaries, the old ruling class and the new, who whatever their differences and their conflicts can be depended upon to go on exploiting the creatures on whose backs they live, and even, as at the end of the story, to unite against them. Orwell is opposing here more than the Soviet or Stalinist experience. In a profound way, both the consciousness of the workers and the possibility of authentic revolution are denied.

These denials, I would say, are inhuman. But it is part of the paradox of Orwell that from this despairing base he is able to generate an immediate and practical humanity: the comradeship of the suffering, which he feels very deeply, and also, more actively, the critical scepticism of the exploited, an unexpected kind of consciousness which informs the story. I have said that *Animal Farm* is unique among Orwell's books because it contains no Orwell figure, no isolated man who breaks from conformity but is then defeated and reabsorbed. This figure is, rather, projected into a collective action: this is what happens to the animals who free themselves and then, through violence and fraud, are again enslaved.

The collective projection has a further effect. What happens is a common rather than an isolated experience, for all its bitterness. The whine of ragged nerves, the despair of a lonely trajectory, are replaced by an active communication which is the tone of the critical narrative. A paradoxical confidence, an assured and active and laughing intelligence, is manifested in the very penetration and exposure of the experience of defeat. Through this very particular mode, Orwell is able to release an exceptionally strong and pure prose. 'All animals are equal ... but some are more equal than others.' It is not surprising that this has passed into ordinary language with a meaning much stronger than the simple satire on revolutionary betrayal. It is one of those permanent statements about the gap between pretence and actuality, profession and practice, over a very wide range. In many places through *Animal Farm* this strong and liberating intelligence transforms a bitter perception into an active and stimulating critique. Beyond the details of the local analogy, and paradoxically beyond the more fundamental despair, this lively awareness connects and informs. Even the last sad scene, where the excluded animals look from man to pig and pig to man and cannot tell which is which, carries a feeling that is more than disillusion and defeat. Seeing that they are the same because they act the same, never mind the labels and the formalities: that is a moment of gained consciousness, a potentially liberating discovery. In its small scale and within its limited terms, *Animal Farm* has a radical energy which goes far beyond its occasion and has its own kind of permanence.

Nineteen Eighty-Four is obviously very different. The curve of isolated feelings, of a ragged and breathless exposure, has returned and is decisive. Yet there are still many elements of the novel which belong to a more liberating consciousness. The appendix, 'The Principles of Newspeak', was never fully incorporated in the imaginative world, but its central perception of a relation between linguistic and social forms is powerful: 'the special function of certain Newspeak words, of which *oldthink* was one, was not so much to express meanings as to destroy them' (NEF, 311). Some Newspeak words—*prolefeed, speedwise, sexcrime*—have already, a generation later, an ominously familiar sound. So too have the names of new government departments: in Newspeak, Minitrue, Minipax, Miniluv, and Miniplenty. I would expect that the copywriters of Mintech were admirers of Orwell, but if they had read him they had certainly not understood him. Much of the jargon of 'modernisation'—that extraordinary substitute for social democracy which the British Labour Government adopted and propagated in the sixties—is almost wholly Newspeak. Some of the techniques of news management sound similarly familiar. The Fiction Department, as an institution, would now hardly even be noticed. And when Winston Smith describes a typical film show—'the helicopter planted a 20 kilo bomb in among them terrific flash and the boat went all to matchwood. Then there was a wonderful shot of a child's arm going up up up right up into the air a helicopter with a camera in its nose must have followed it up' (NEF, 12)—it is as if he had seen the television newsreels from Vietnam; only the weight of the bomb is an absurd underestimate.

Again, in a rather different way, 'Big Brother Is Watching You' has also made its way into ordinary language, as the motto of a sceptical resistance. In these very simple and powerful ways Orwell succeeded in articulating certain quite evident elements of our prolonged social crisis. As an intransigent enemy of every kind of *thoughtcrime* and *doublethink*, Orwell is still very close and alive.

His vision of power politics is also close and convincing. The transposition of official 'allies' and 'enemies' has happened, almost openly, in the generation since he wrote. His idea of a world divided into three blocs— Oceania, Eurasia, and Eastasia, of which two are always at war with the third though the alliances change, is again too close for comfort. And there are times when one can believe that what 'had been called England or Britain' has become simply Airstrip One.

With these elements of the projection so recognisable, at least in their general outlines, it is necessary to ask why so much else is so wrong. It is significant that Orwell took his model of a controlled and military society from Soviet communism, even including detailed elements of its past such as the conflict between Stalin and Trotsky (Big Brother and Goldstein). The ideology of Airstrip One is Ingsoc—English socialism—and when the book became a success in the United States he had to issue a denial that this related to the postwar Labour Government:

> My recent novel is NOT intended as an attack on Socialism or on the British Labour Party (of which I am a supporter) but as a show-up of the perversions to which a centralised economy is liable and which have already been partly realised in Communism and Fascism. (CEJL, IV, 502)

Ingsoc, it might then be said, is no more English Socialism than Minitrue is the Ministry of Truth. But the identification was in effect made, and has been profoundly damaging. Not in what it says about Soviet society—Orwell's position there was clear and consistent

—but in what it implied generally about socialism and a 'centralised economy'. This connects with the most evident error in Orwell's projection : that the permanent and controlled war economy is shabby and under-supplied. The structural relations, that we can now see, between a militarist economy and a controlled consumer affluence amount to more than a historical development which Orwell did not foresee. They indicate some of the social facts which, in what became an obsession with ideology, he did not take account of. There are good reasons why Orwell might not have foreseen an affluent and militarist capitalism, or a world of international corporations which function, internally and externally, very much like his projected Party. But he had the best of reasons—in direct experience—for knowing that political police, for example, were not a socialist or communist invention; or propaganda, or censorship, or *agents provocateurs*. By assigning all modern forms of repression and authoritarian control to a single political tendency, he not only misrepresented it, but cut short the kind of analysis that would recognise these inhuman and destructive forces wherever they appeared, under whatever names and masked by whatever ideology. For it would certainly, now, be *doublethink* to suppose that the only source of these elements is a form of socialism, just as it is only *thoughtcrime* that could prevent us from seeing a propaganda phrase like 'the free world' as a very clear example of Newspeak. In projecting a world that is all too recognisable, Orwell confused us about its structures, its ideologies, and the possibilities of resisting it.

This point about resistance has a further importance, when we remember Orwell's earlier work. At the most general level, his projection has undoubtedly been falsified. Under controls as pervasive and as cruel, many men and women have kept faith with each other, have kept their courage, and in several cases against heavy odds have risen to try to destroy the system or to change it. We can write Berlin, Budapest, Algiers, Aden, Wattsville, Prague in the margins of Orwell's passivity. He himself could have written St Petersburg, Kronstadt, Barcelona, Warsaw. It would be right to acknowledge that many of the risings were defeats, but Orwell goes further, cutting out the spring of hope. He projects an enormous apathy on all the oppressed: a created mood, if ever there was one. Eighty-five per cent of the population are seen as an apathetic mass, and *proles*, as a description of them, seems more than Party jargon. The Party sees them as 'natural inferiors ... like animals', but how does Orwell see them? As a shouting, stupid crowd in the streets; drinking and gambling; 'like the ant, which can see small objects but not large ones'; 'people who have never learned to think'. It is the world of working people, before 1914, as seen by the prep-school boy: 'To me in my early boyhood, to nearly all children of families like mine, "common" people seemed almost sub-human' (RWP, 127). But, as in another earlier experience, this 'almost sub-human' world can be seen, in a moment of revulsion from his own class, as the hope of the future, redeemers to be looked at with 'mystical reverence': 'people who had never learned to think but who were storing up in their hearts and bellies and muscles the power that would one day overturn the world' (NEF, 226). 'Out of those mighty loins a race of conscious beings must one day come' (NEF, 227).

This stale revolutionary romanticism is as insulting as the original observation. It is the rising of the animals, as in the fable. 'When you put it in words it sounded reasonable; it was when you looked at the human beings passing you on the pavement that it became an act of faith' (NEF, 89). It needs to be said, however bitterly, that if the tyranny of 1984 ever finally comes, one of the major elements of the ideological preparation will have been just this way of seeing 'the masses', 'the human beings passing you on the pavement', the eighty-five per cent who are *proles*. And nobody who belongs to this majority or who knows them as people will give a damn whether the figure on the other side of the street sees them as animals to be subjected or as unthinking creatures out of those mighty loins the future will come. The incomplete humanity will be too clearly visible in the gesticulating observer himself.

That is how it goes, politically, throughout. Orwell had seen clearly the world of the power blocs, but the 'hundreds of millions of ill-paid and hard-working coolies', inhabiting 'a rough quadrilateral with its corners at Tangier, Brazzaville, Darwin and Hong Kong' (NEF, 192) are also passive: 'If they did not exist, the structure of world society, and the process by which it maintains itself, would not be essentially different' (NEF, 193). It is a dreadful underestimate, not only of those people but of the structures of exploitation through which the metropolitan states are sustained. By viewing the struggle as one between only a few people over the heads of an apathetic mass, Orwell created the conditions for defeat and despair.

He continues his underestimate. He had seen people go back into Spain, under the threat of arrest, because of general and particular loyalties. He had seen hundreds of cases of fidelity under pressure. His wife had stayed in Barcelona, even lying in bed while the police searched her room, to be near him and to help him. But still

> Under the spreading chestnut tree
> I sold you and you sold me.

He can describe this accurately as 'a peculiar, cracked, braying, jeering note ... a yellow note' (NEF, 81), but still it is what he makes happen. The cynical jingle of the rat-race, which in similar forms we have been hearing ever since from the agency offices and parties, leads straight to the nightmare of the rat in Room 101. Of course people break down under torture, but not all people break down. And in a filthy and repressive world there are deeper forms of personal resistance—as Orwell had reason to know—than the temporary affair between Winston and Julia.

The Party campaign against sex is one of the stranger elements of the projection (that it seems to have been taken from Zamyatin's *We* is relevant but secondary). The object of the campaign is to prevent uncontrollable loyalties but even more to 'remove all pleasure from the sexual act'. There have been such campaigns, though in some exploiting systems the first purpose can be achieved by a kind of abstract reversal of the second: pleasure without loyalty is even a marketable and institutional commodity. It is strange that Orwell could oppose the controls and the perversions with nothing better than the casual affair between Winston and Julia. This begins like the lovemaking trip to the country in *Keep the Aspidistra Flying*, but then it moves right away from any mutually recognising personal experience:

> His heart leapt. Scores of times she had done it: he wished it had been hundreds—thousands. Anything that hinted at corruption always filled him with a wild hope. (NEF, 129)

It is not the ordinary and continuing love of men and women, in friendship and in marriage, but a willed corruption or indifference—'the simple undifferentiated desire'—that is presented as opposed to (though it is usually part of) that joyless world. Winston's marriage is a cold and miserable routine; only with the hint of corruption can the pleasure come.

Of the many failures in *Nineteen Eighty-Four* this is perhaps the deepest. All the ordinary resources of personal life are written off as summarily as the *proles*. The lonely fantasy of 'mighty loins' of the future is joined by the lonely confusion of the adolescent—so guilty about lovemaking that corruption of the object is a necessary element of its pleasure. Winston Smith is not like a man at all—in consciousness, in relationships, in the capacity for love and protection and endurance and loyalty. He is the last of the cut-down figures—less experienced, less intelligent, less loyal, less courageous than his creator—through whom rejection and defeat can be mediated.

The question about the view of the future in *Nineteen Eighty-Four* is not an abstract one concerning a change from the optimism of Mercier or Wells to the pessimism of Huxley or Orwell. Abstract optimism and pessimism are almost equally beside the point, and there are plausible grounds for seeing a generalised future that is either dark or bright. What matters much more than the imposed general mood is the amount of experience that is drawn on. Promises or warnings that limit experience have limited relevance. So the question about *Nineteen Eighty-Four*, as about Orwell's earlier novels, is why he created situations and people that, in comparison with his own written observations, are one-dimensional and determined. This is not primarily a matter of politics, but of a more extended experience of self and society.

Under the strength and sense of his only successful character, 'Orwell'—a man physically and intellectually alive and conscious and tough and persistent—moved these feebler and less conscious figures in an undifferentiated theatrical landscape. The central significance is not in the personal contradictions but in the much deeper structures of a society and its literature. In making his projections, Orwell expressed much more than himself.

7 Continuities

Soon after his death Orwell became, in effect, a symbolic figure. He was one of those men whose life and writing were in practice inseparable, and who seemed to offer a style in which others could live and write. It would be easy to say that this was because he was a disillusioned, decent, and plain-living anti-communist : a figure the age needed. Of course the promotion of this image took place, but most people who had read him saw past it. It is significant that he was not respected only by people who had given up their commitment to radical social change and who were using Orwell's disillusion as a cover. There were plenty of these, and others who didn't even have to live the process through, who could take Orwell's disillusion neat. But there were just as many who began their political commitment from the point where Orwell left off, who agreed with him about Stalinism and about imperialism and about the English establishment, and who made a new socialist politics out of his sense of a failure.

There is a clear line, certainly, from Orwell's 'Inside the Whale' and *Nineteen Eighty-Four* to an orthodox North Atlantic mood in which all humane and positive beliefs, and especially a belief in radical change, can be recognised in advance as either a projection of some personal or social maladjustment, or as an inexperienced, naïve, adolescent idealism, which despite the will and vision of its bearers leads in practice straight to the authoritarianism which more sinister figures are all the time preparing, behind this apparently innocent front. These explanations and warnings are still being confidently offered, sometimes with Orwell's name attached, as to the student movements of the past few years. Again, in some relation to this, there is certainly a clear line from Orwell's social thinking in 'The Lion and the Unicorn' and similar essays to the British Labour Party revisionists of the fifties and sixties. Their definition of socialism as the pursuit of equality had a traditional sound but a more precise contemporary significance: what had been understood as a socialist economy was (they argued) outdated by the development of an affluent industrial society; a new classlessness was emerging of its own accord and would be confirmed by measures of pragmatic social reform. Or, in Orwell's terms, the 'wrong members of the family', the old 'feudal' or 'aristocratic' elements, would be displaced by the new men, the 'new Britain', and then the nation would become more civilised, more humane, more generally and equitably prosperous—just what Orwell had wanted as far back as *The Road to Wigan Pier*. This relates to the feeling held by radicals who were not directly involved in the political arguments that Orwell, unlike other socialist writers, understood English life—its pace, its tolerance, its distrust of abstractions and of any theory pushed to extremes: a sensible, moderate, decent kind of life, which any hurried or drastic changes would disturb or put at risk, but which was still the basis for a steady extension of humane and responsible living.

We could call these views and moods Orwell's inheritance. But it is then all the more remarkable that the generation for whom Suez, Hungary, and the Bomb were signals for the renewal of political action looked to him with respect; a generation that believed not only in a new socialist movement, but one based on disturbance: on demonstrations, on direct action, on the politics of the streets and the localities. This New Left respected Orwell directly, especially in its early years. The invasion of Suez was an open exercise of the British Imperialism he had so consistently attacked. The Hungarian revolution, a popular and socialist rising against a bureaucratic and authoritarian communism, was at once a confirmation of what he had said about Stalinism and a demonstration of the authentic movement to which he had paid homage in Catalonia. The danger of the Bomb —'either we renounce it or it destroys us'—was as he had seen it: not only the weapon which could destroy civilisation, but the shadow under which a new authoritarian war economy would grow and extend. And then, closely involved with these political positions, there was the Orwell who had written about work, about poverty, about popular culture, the Orwell who had tried to live and feel where the majority of English people were living and feeling: reporting, understanding, respecting, beyond the range of an Establishment culture. These discernible elements of the New Left in Britain are, equally clearly, Orwell's effective inheritance.

What kind of phenomenon is this, then, when the same man, the same writer, symbolises such different tendencies, is appealed to and respected by opposing groups? It would be easy but pointless to start a quarrel over Orwell's inheritance: body-snatching or mantle-snatching; a figure or a style to dignify his reputed successors. No useful analysis can go in for that. There has been too much of it already, in everything from anecdote to impersonation. 'Father Knew George Orwell' is a cracked old song.

Nor is it very useful to attempt some reductive analy-

sis. It would be easy to say that these different tendencies can be explained chronologically: the thirties
Orwell is the socialist, the forties Orwell the reactionary,
the radical somewhere in between. But I have looked
carefully through his writings, considering this explanation, and I am sure it doesn't work. Evidence for each of
the positions can be drawn from each of the periods,
though of course with differences of emphasis. There is
the anti-imperialist of the early thirties, the revolutionary socialist of the late thirties, the radical essayist of the
late thirties and forties. Yet in the same periods there are
the patterns of defeat, the figure of the isolated honest
man who has seen beyond the socialist talk, and the
propagation of the myths of England. Or there is the
disillusioned and embittered prophet of the forties, seeing progress as a swindle and revolution as self-defeating,
but this man is also the radical essayist of the *Tribune*
articles, active not only in defence of the victims of
Stalinism but also in defence of 'the civil liberties of any
citizens of the British Empire', even including, past his
doubts and reservations, a man convicted for passing
atomic secrets to the USSR (CEJL, IV, 197, 377). That
there are phases of Orwell's development is clear enough,
but within each period there are some of the same contradictions.

A reductive analysis by forms of writing may again
seem plausible but does not really work. Most radicals, I
have noticed, prefer his essays, as if 'The Art of Donald
McGill' or 'Dickens' or 'How the Poor Die' or 'Raffles and
Miss Blandish' were somehow his major works. I admire
these and many of the other essays, but I don't believe
they can be isolated from his other work, and an Orwell
restricted to them would be a very much smaller figure.
Or take the novels, up to *Coming Up for Air*. They have

been much more influential than has been commonly noticed; indeed one could say they created the style of the drifting anti-hero English novel of the fifties, though themselves based on such diverse sources as Wells and Joyce, Gissing and Somerset Maugham. But the point is that all the contradictory tendencies are in the novels: the colloquial style and the seeking-out of ordinary life, but also the patterns of defeat, self-hatred, and that generalised swearing which covers reabsorption. In the journals and reporting there is usually a stronger and more consistent position, but some of the basic ambiguities are evident in almost everything but *Homage to Catalonia*. The creation of 'Orwell'—the honest observer —is more successful than the creation of the fictional characters, but we still have to explain the contradictions in that central consciousness.

Indeed the contradictions, the paradox of Orwell, must be seen as paramount. Instead of flattening out the contradictions by choosing this or that tendency as the 'real' Orwell, or fragmenting them by separating this or that period or this or that genre, we ought to say that it is the paradoxes which are finally significant. No simple explanation of them will do justice to so complex a man (the more complex because he appears, on the surface, so plain). Some of the concepts we need for any full explanation may be beyond our reach just because of what we share with Orwell: a particular kind of historical pressure, a particular structure of responses and failures to respond. But two points can be suggested.

First, the key to Orwell as an individual is the problem of identity. Educated as he was to a particular consciousness, the key to his whole development is that he renounced it, or attempted to renounce it, and that he made a whole series of attempts to find a new social identity. Because of this process, we have a writer who was successively many things that would be unlikely in a normal trajectory: an imperial police officer, a resident of a casual ward, a revolutionary militiaman, a declassed intellectual, a middle-class English writer. And the strength of his work is that in the energy of his renunciation he was exceptionally open to each new experience as it came. Different kinds of life flowed through him with only a minimal check from a more established identity, and the style he evolved—a studied simplicity, 'letting the meaning choose the word'—shows that while always travelling seriously, he was always travelling light. This quality can be related to his willingness to renounce his earlier attitudes and experiences and to write about them—or about others now in them—with contempt or anger, as if they were some other, quite separated thing. Yet in a period of exceptional mobility, this has positive as well as negative elements. Orwell could connect as closely and with as many different kinds of people as he did, precisely because of his continual mobility, his successive and serious assumption of roles. When he is in a situation, he is so dissolved into it that he is exceptionally convincing, and his kind of writing makes it easy for the reader to believe that this is also happening to himself. The absence of roots is also the absence of barriers.

It would be possible to say that this is the writer's 'negative capability' of which Keats wrote. But there is no permanent psychology of 'the writer'. This is the social psychology of a particular kind of writer in a particular epoch. It is even, in Orwell's period, a class psychology: Aldous Huxley, W. H. Auden, Graham Greene, Christopher Isherwood, for all their differences, share with Orwell important elements of this position:

travelling light and often, which is their overt social history; realising others—other lives but especially other beliefs, other attitudes, other moods—through their own shifting negations. This structure of feeling is not what Keats meant by 'negative capability'; it is at once sharper and smaller. The clarity and memorability of the successive realisations are an undoubted achievement, but there is also a characteristic coldness, an inability to realise the full life of another, seeing the other instead as a figure in an unrolling private landscape. In the case of Orwell, this coldness is most evident in his novels, where the presence of another as someone more than a stranger met or seen on a journey is expected and does not come. Relationships are characteristically meagre, ephemeral, reluctant, disillusioning, even betraying, and this is very remarkable in the work of so generous a man. But one is reminded, very sharply, that in this at least Orwell was writing with the grain of his time. The relationships in his novels are characteristic relationships in the fiction of a period—a period marked by the certainty, even dogma, that this, now, is what all relationships are like. This is what I meant in saying that to describe the paradox of Orwell we would need concepts beyond the consciousness and the social structures of his period. All we can now propose is experience: that there are other, fuller, more continuing relationships; that there are ways beyond even this alienation.

Yet Orwell tried again and again to affirm, putting his life on the line. That is what makes him much more than a passive figure in this dominant structure of feeling. He shared it, but he tried to transcend it. As clearly as anyone in his generation, he sensed that this was, after all, a historical crisis, not a human condition or a metaphysical fact. His mobility, then, had a clear social intention.

He was travelling light, but it was sureness of instinct, not chance, that took him to all the critical places and experiences of his epoch; and he was not only a visitor, either, but a man wanting and hoping to join in. He made a single life contain, at first hand, the experiences of imperialism, of revolution, of poverty. He had no theory to explain them and no rooted positive beliefs extending beyond his own role. But with great stubbornness and persistence and courage he went to the centres of the history that was determining him, so that it might be experienced and differently determined. This, above everything, was his individual achievement. He was the writer who put himself out, who kept going and taking part, and who learned to write as a function of this very precise exploration.

But it is therefore more than an individual history. Nobody who shared or overlapped with his epoch can, in good faith, reduce his crisis to a personal development. There were important personal factors in his successes and in his failures, but some of the deepest contradictions are part of a shared history, and we cannot set ourselves above it, as if he were an abstract critical problem.

The second key to an understanding is, then, the nature of capitalist democracy in an epoch of socialist revolutions, of imperialism, of fascism, and of war. In the thirties it was not difficult to see capitalist democracy in the context of political imperialism and economic depression. Its complicity with fascism, or at best its willingness to deal with fascism in a common opposition to socialism, could be seen not only in its dealings with the Soviet Union but in Spain. Reservations could be made about the nature of Soviet communism, or the internal politics of the Spanish Republic, yet a set of bearings held, or for many years seemed to hold. Capitalist democracy would not fight fascism, any more than it would liberate the colonial peoples or end the poverty which disfigured it in its own societies. Socialism had its profound internal differences and its own deep distortions, but it was the name, everywhere, for opposition to that dangerous and exploiting alliance.

Under massive historical pressures, in a very intricate process of cause and effect, this world view was profoundly modified. The development of revolution in the Soviet Union and in Spain was itself deeply and bitterly affected by the character of the alliance against it and by its own desperate need for survival. Within a few years, what had seemed impossible became inescapable history: not only the further degeneration of Soviet communism in the Stalin trials, and the betrayal of Spain, which were bitter enough, but the world-altering events of 1939: the pact between Stalin and Hitler and the beginning of war between fascism and the capitalist democracies. It may be easier, now, to gain some perspective on this process: to see the shadow of the incredible in the long earlier history of betrayal and default, the submerged contradictions coming at last into the open.

But it is not only the shock of those years that is important. The most important effect, for anyone in Orwell's position, was the consequent response to capitalist democracy, for it was here that, beyond the old contradictions and illusions, new contradictions and illusions were being laid down almost unnoticed. For Orwell the physical inevitability of the war against fascism combined first, as we have seen, with a traditional attachment to his country: Orwell's mature myth of England was written at just this point. But it was not just England that was in question, but the nature of capitalist democracy. In adjusting to England, and to the war against fascism, it was easy to over-adjust. 'Capitalist', as a qualification of 'democracy', could in effect be omitted or its reality underestimated, as it was in the illusion that the war against Germany could be turned into a revolutionary war, or as in the deeper, much more persistent illusion that it would be possible, quite quickly and without major disturbance, to bring the real England—democratic England—to the surface, breaking through the thin upper crust of an exhausted and archaic system. To the extent that 'democracy' could be isolated, as in the alliance against fascism seemed plausible, it could be made the basis of an unanswerable criticism of a socialist order which under long historical pressures had become authoritarian. This would not have made so much sense if the experience of democracy had not been real : both in the inheritance of a liberal capitalism, and in the bitterly fought-for freedoms of what was in effect a popular and anti-capitalist culture. Physically it was there, its radically diverse elements confused and apparently inextricable. But in isolating the contrast between democratic and authoritarian regimes, abstracting them from the developing and contradictory character of their real social systems, a new set of illusions, a new and historically fragile world-view, was in fact prepared. This was, indeed, similar, in structure and effect, to the earlier isolation and abstraction of 'socialism'.

In other West European countries, where elements of the old order collaborated with fascism and new alliances had to be made in the necessary resistance, other choices were possible. But in England capitalist democracy survived with its main contradictions intact, and then the pretence or hope that it was social democracy, or was about to become so, lasted longer than was good

for anybody's reason. Even after the profound disillu-
sions of 1945–51 and 1964–70, the pretence or hope survived. Yet no such illusion is static. If the only effective
social contrast was between 'democracy' and 'communism', then some sort of accommodation with capitalism
—that capitalism which was 'on the point of' becoming
a social democracy—was at first temporarily and then
habitually conceivable. Having made this accommodation, and the corresponding identification of 'communism' as the sole threat, it became harder to see and to
admit what capitalist imperialism was still capable of
doing: what, in the years since Orwell died, it has done
again and again, in repression and in war.

This is the knot that was tied in the middle 1940s. And
Orwell, indeed, helped to tie it. Then in his last fiction he
discarded the apparently positive element of the illusion—the belief in the imminence of social democracy—
and was left with only its negative effects. He could see
only authoritarian communism in the future, with no
alternative or countervailing social forces. The first proposed title for what became *Nineteen Eighty-Four* was
The Last Man in Europe, and that is clearly how it felt. It
has a certain bleak honesty, but it reveals a point at
which the political contradictions, and the isolation and
abstraction involved in them, combined with the lack of
any independent social identity to produce a genuine
terror.

This would not have got through to so many people if
the contradictions had not been so general. But what in
Orwell was a last desperate throw became for many
others, absurdly, a way of life. His radical pessimism
was combined with an accommodation to capitalism
and with an illusion of the imminence of social democracy. What in Orwell broke down in terror became

a comfortable and persistent world view (in an older generation even lasting beyond Vietnam).

The only useful thing, now, is to understand how it happened. In a confused and mobile history, his kind of loss of identity has continued to occur. The affiliation he tried to make, that he was ready to die for, was prevented by the political contradictions of those years and was lost, finally, in illusion and terror. The writer had to split from the political militant. Faith in the people had to be projected to an evolutionary distance : much farther than would ever have been necessary if his original class idea of unthinking sub-humans had not translated so easily into a disillusioned view of the apathetic and tolerant mass. Beyond and past him, in and through many of the contradictions he experienced, real popular forces have continued to move, and the fight he joined and then despaired of has been renewed, has extended, and has gained important new ground.

We are never likely to reach a time when we can do without his frankness, his energy, his willingness to join in. These are the qualities we shall go on respecting in him, whatever other conclusions we may come to. But they are real qualities only if they are independent and active. The thing to do with his work, his history, is to read it, not imitate it. He is still there, tangibly, with the wound in his throat, the sad strong face, the plain words written in hardship and exposure. But then as we reach out to touch him we catch something of his hardness, a necessary hardness. We are acknowledging a presence and a distance : other names, other years; a history to respect, to remember, to move on from.

AFTERWORD: *Nineteen Eighty-Four* in 1984

I

It was never at all likely that any actual society, in 1984, would much resemble the hellhole of Orwell's novel. He was in any case not making that kind of prediction:

> I do not believe that the kind of society I describe necessarily *will* arrive, but I believe (allowing of course for the fact that the book is a satire) that something resembling it *could* arrive. (CEJL, IV, 502)

The qualification is important. He had written earlier:

> This is a novel about the future – that is, it is in a sense a fantasy, but in the form of a naturalistic novel. That is what makes it a difficult job – of course as a book of anticipations it would be comparatively simple to write. (CEJL, IV, 329–30)

This difficulty of the form needs emphasis, as we try in his arbitrarily dated year to reassess his vision. The form is in fact more complex than the combination, in his terms, of 'fantasy' and 'naturalistic novel'. For there is a third element, most clearly represented by the extracts from the notorious Book and by the appendix on 'The Principles of Newspeak'. In the case of the Book, especially, the method of the writing is that of argument: the historical and political essay.

There are then in effect three layers in the novel.

First, an infrastructure, immediately recognisable from Orwell's other fiction, in which the hero-victim moves through a squalid world in a series of misunderstandings and disappointments, trying and failing to hold on to the possibility – as much a memory as a vision – of a sweeter kind of life. Second, a structure of argument, indeed of anticipations, in the extracts from the Book and in some of the more general descriptions of the actual society. Third, a superstructure, including many of the most memorable elements, in which, by a method ranging from fantasy to satire and parody, the cruelty and repression of the society are made to appear at once ludicrous and savagely absurd.

The three levels are of course interconnected, though, as he recognised, imperfectly. The figure of the hero-victim is connected because at the centre of his memory or vision is an idea of truth, which the social order is determined to destroy. The everyday squalor is more generally connected, in the argument that the state of perpetual war has been instituted to keep people poor, but also as a bitter reversal of the normal condition of the authoritarian Utopia, in which material plenty is commonplace. Similarly, the most bizarre elements of the superstructure – the spy telescreen, Newspeak, the memory hole, the Two Minutes Hate, the Anti-Sex League – are satirical projections of the state of mind of the central social order:

> I believe . . . that totalitarian ideas have taken root in the minds of intellectuals everywhere, and I have tried to draw these ideas out to their logical consequences. (CEJL, IV, 502)

As for the passages of argument, Orwell strongly resisted a suggestion from an American publisher that they should be abridged.

> It would alter the whole colour of the book and leave out a good deal that is essential. (CEJL, IV, 483)

He made the same point in commenting on a draft blurb from his English publisher:

> It makes the book sound as though it were a thriller mixed up with a love story, and I didn't intend it to be primarily that. What it is really meant to do is to discuss the implications of dividing the world up into 'Zones of influence' (I thought of it in 1944 as a result of the Teheran conference), and in addition to indicate by parodying them the intellectual implications of totalitarianism. (CEJL, IV, 460)

It is then from Orwell's own sense of the book that we can find support for taking this central structure of argument, this element of reasoned anticipation, as important. Moreover it is above all with this central structure that a re-reading in 1984 should be primarily concerned.

This is so in spite of some formal difficulties, which can be briefly noted. Writing under great difficulties, because of his illness, Orwell undoubtedly had problems in integrating these levels of argument. This is especially clear in the fact that the essay on 'The Principles of Newspeak' had to be put in as an appendix, though some of it is a more developed version of the description and examples he had included in the main narrative. It is one of Orwell's liveliest essays, but there is a problem of position, caused by its attachment to the story. Thus within the first two pages Orwell veers between a position as historian of Ingsoc and Newspeak –

> It is with the final, perfected version, as embodied in the Eleventh Edition of the Dictionary, that we are concerned here (NEF, 305)

– and a position as contemporary essayist, contemplating the horrible projection –

> Newspeak was founded on the English language as we now know it, though many Newspeak sentences, even when not containing newly created words, would be barely intelligible to an Englishspeaker of our own day. (NEF, 306)

This kind of uncertainty, in fact soon overcome by the interest of the examples, is repeated in a more serious way in the extracts from the Book. On the one hand, as will be shown, they are very close to some of Orwell's own political thinking at the time, and even closer to some of his more obvious sources. They are in any case presented as from the secret Book of the underground opposition, the Brotherhood, and as written by the reviled Goldstein. On the other hand, like so much else that at first sight appears hopeful and trustworthy, they are eventually presented as elements of the Party's total deception. The Inner Party torturer O'Brien says:

> 'I wrote it. That is to say, I collaborated in writing it. No book is produced individually, as you know.'
> 'Is it true, what it says?'

'As description, yes. The programme it sets forth is nonsense.' (NEF, 267)

The intricacies of deception and betrayal, and of the deliberate confusion of truth and lies, are at this point so great that it is futile to ask which version Orwell intended readers to believe. What matters much more is that the extracts are there – whatever the plausibility of their use in an already complete trap – because Orwell wanted to set out, in a consecutive argument, his ideas of how the world was going and could go. The narrative status of the Book becomes important only when we compare his fictional projections, in the extracts and in the more general story, with what he was writing in the same years without these special problems of form.

Three themes predominate in this central structure on which, at the level of ideas, the book is founded. First, there is the division of the world into three super-states, which in shifting alliances are in a state of limited but perpetual war. Second, there is the internal tyranny of each of these states, with a specific version of the relations between social classes and a detailed presentation of a totalitarian society which has been developed beyond both capitalism and socialism. Third, there is the exceptional emphasis on the control of a society through ideas and means of communication: backed up by direct repression and torture but mainly operating through 'thought control'.

These three themes need to be considered in detail, both in Orwell's presentation of them and in the actual history to which they offer to relate. It is especially important to consider all three, and to see how Orwell thought of them as essentially interrelated. Ironically, however, it is only possible to consider them, with the seriousness that he expected, if we isolate them, temporarily, from the actual structure of the novel, and, in a more permanent way, from the resonance which, since its publication, has surrounded it.

It would be possible, for example, to run a silly kind of checklist on the projections. Is there an Anti-Sex League? Is there a two-way telescreen for spying on people in their homes? Is there a statutory Two Minutes Hate? No? Well then it just shows, as some said at the time, that the book is a wild kind of horror-comic, or at best stupidly exaggerated. But these are elements of the parodic superstructure. The structure then? Yet in the predominant political resonance which has surrounded the novel we do not even have to look at these arguments, because their proof is already given in the real world. 'This is where socialism gets you.' 'This is where it has already got, in Russia and Eastern Europe.' But Orwell was quick to separate himself from this interpretation, which accounted for much of the early success of the book and which is still offered as if it were beyond question.

> My recent novel is NOT intended as an attack on Socialism or on the British Labour Party (of which I am a supporter) but as a show-up of the perversions to which a centralised economy is liable and which have already been partly realised in Communism and Fascism. (CEJL, IV, 502)

'*Partly* realised', in the social orders directed by Stalin and Hitler. The full perversions are shown as going further. Moreover the easy response, to put down the book and look East, where 'it is all already happening', should be checked by Orwell's emphasis:

> The scene of the book is laid in Britain in order to emphasise that the English-speaking races are not innately better than anyone else and that totalitarianism, *if not fought against*, could triumph anywhere. (CEJL, IV, 502)

The point is more than one of local correction, against the use and abuse of the novel during the cold war. It is central to Orwell's arguments that what is being described, in its main tendencies, is not only a universal danger but a universal process. That is the true source of his horror. If the novel is absorbed into the propaganda of this or that state, as a basis for hating and fearing an enemy state, against which there must be preparation for war, there is the really savage irony that a citizen of Oceania, in 1984, is thinking as he has been programmed to think, but with the reassurance of the book to tell him that he is free and that only those others are propagandised and brainwashed. Orwell was offering no such reassurance. He saw the super-states, the spy states, and the majority populations controlled by induced ideas as the way *the world* was going, to the point where there would still be arbitrary enemies, and names and figures to hate, but where there would be no surviving faculty of discovering or telling the truth about *our own* situation: the situation of any of us, in any of the states and alliances. This is a much harder position than any simple anti-socialism or anti-communism. It is indeed so hard that we must begin by examining what he took to be its overpowering conditions, leading first to the super-states and to limited perpetual war.

II

Nineteen Eighty-Four is so often quoted as a vision of the worst possible future world that it may seem odd to say that in at least one respect Orwell notably underestimated a general danger. It is not often remembered that in the novel a war with atomic bombs has been fought in the 1950s. There are not many details, though it is mentioned that an atomic bomb fell on Colchester. This is one of several instances in which, read from the actual 1984, the novel can be clearly seen as belonging to the 1940s. Orwell was quick to comment on the importance of the new weapon. He wrote in *Tribune* in October 1945 that it was dangerous mainly because it made the strong much stronger; its difficult manufacture meant that it would be reserved to a few powerful societies that were already heavily industrialised. 'The great age of democracy and of national self-determination' had been 'the age of the musket and the rifle'. Now, with this invention,

> we have before us the prospect of two or three monstrous super-states, each possessed of a weapon by which millions of people can be wiped out in a few seconds, dividing the world between them. (CEJL, IV, 8)

This is not only the outline of the world of *Nineteen Eighty-Four*. It is also an intelligent recognition of the actual power of the new weapons. Yet still, after this, he included in his story a war with atomic weapons after which, though with its own kinds of horror, a relatively recognisable land and society survived. This is no discredit to Orwell. Again and again it has been almost impossible to imagine the true consequences of an atomic *war*, as distinct from the one-sided use of the bomb which has been the only actual event. Indeed there has been a familiar kind of *doublethink* about nuclear weapons, in which it is simultaneously if contradictorily known that they would lead to massive and in many cases absolute destruction and yet that, with sufficient political determination, of whatever kind, they could be absorbed and survived.

The idea of an atomic war in the 1950s was common enough in the middle and late 1940s. It was seen as virtually inevitable, once more than one state possessed atomic bombs, by several writers and especially by James Burnham, about whom Orwell wrote two substantial essays in the years in which he was writing *Nineteen Eighty-Four*. Orwell began his novel in August 1946 and completed the first draft in November 1947. His essay 'Burnham and the Managerial Revolution' was published in May 1946 and 'Burnham and the Contemporary World Struggle' in March 1947. The essays are full of the themes of the novel, and there are several close correspondences between them and the fictional extracts from the Book. On the other hand there are significant differences between Orwell's discriminating discussions of Burnham's theses and the relatively simplified presentation of closely comparable ideas in the Book.

Thus Burnham's argument in *The Struggle for the World* is that the United States, while in sole possession of the atomic bomb, should move to prevent any other nation ever acquiring it. Orwell comments that 'he is demanding, or all but demanding, an immediate preventive war against Russia' (CEJL, IV, 316), and indeed such proposals, to be preceded by ultimatum-like demands to abandon 'communism' or 'world-communism', were directly made by others. Against such arguments, Orwell in the later essay hoped that there would be more time than Burnham had supposed: 'perhaps ten years, but more probably only five' (CEJL, IV, 314). If there was indeed more time there would be better political directions than an American world order and an anti-communist crusade. He added that 'the more the pessimistic world-view of Burnham and others like him prevails, the harder it is for such [alternative] ideas to take hold' (CEJL, IV, 324).

It is strange now, when Burnham has been largely forgotten, and when *Nineteen Eighty-Four* is so much better known than Orwell's essays, to retrace the formation of the 'pessimistic world-view' of the novel. We can look again at the idea of the dominant super-states. In the novel it is as follows:

> The splitting up of the world into three great super-states was an event which could be and indeed was foreseen before the middle of the twentieth century. With the absorption of Europe by Russia and of the British Empire by the United States, two of the three existing powers, Eurasia and Oceania, were already effectively in being. The third, Eastasia, only emerged as a distinct unit after another decade of confused fighting. (NEF, 190)

This is more or less directly taken from Burnham:

Burnham's geographical picture of the new world has turned out to be correct. More and more obviously the surface of the earth is being parcelled off into three great empires, each self-contained and cut off from contact with the outer world, and each ruled, under one disguise or another, by a self-elected oligarchy. (CEJL, IV, 8–9)

The idea is now so familiar, from the novel, that some effort is needed to realise the strangeness of Orwell's assertion, at that date, that the picture 'has turned out to be correct', and, further, that the empire nearest home – the American/British of the fictional Oceania – is, like the more frequently cited Soviet empire, 'ruled ... by a self-elected oligarchy'.

The next stage in Orwell's development of the idea, while he was in the middle of writing his novel, follows from his definition of three political possibilities: a preventive war by the United States, which would be a crime and would in any case solve nothing; a cold war until several nations have atomic bombs, then almost at once a war which would wipe out industrial civilisation and leave only a small population living by subsistence agriculture; or

that the fear inspired by the atomic bomb and other weapons yet to come will be so great that everyone will refrain from using them. This seems to me the worst possibility of all. It would mean the division of the world among two or three vast super-states, unable to conquer one another and unable to be overthrown by any internal rebellion. In all probability their structure would be hierarchic, with a semi-divine caste at the top and outright slavery at the bottom, and the crushing out of liberty would exceed anything that the world has yet seen. Within each state the necessary psychological atmosphere would be kept up by complete severance from the outer world, and by a continuous phony war against rival states. Civilisations of this type might remain static for thousands of years. (CEJL, IV, 371)

This is, in effect, the option taken by the novel, though an intervening and less damaging atomic war has been retained from earlier positions. In his directly political writing, at this time, Orwell saw an alternative to all three dangers: the building of 'democratic Socialism . . . throughout some large area . . . A Socialist United States of Europe seems to me the only worthwhile political objective today' (CEJL, IV, 371). But in the perspective of the fiction this is entirely absent.

Obviously we must ask, in 1984, why none of Orwell's three (or four) possibilities has occurred. Yet we must do this soberly, since we shall not be released from any of the dangers he and others foresaw by the mere passage of a fictional date. It is not, in some jeering way, to prove Orwell wrong, but to go on learning the nature of the historical developments which at his most serious he was trying desperately to understand, that we have to ask what he left out, or what he wrongly included, in his assessment of the world-political future.

First we have to notice that what came through, in this period, were not unitary super-states or empires but the more complex forms of military superpowers and primarily military alliances. There are times, especially as we listen to war propaganda, when we can suppose that the Burnham/Orwell vision has been realised, in the monolithically presented entities of 'East' and 'West', and with China as the shifting partner of either. But the full political realities have turned out to be very different. There is, for example, a coexistent and different hierarchy of *economic* power, with Japan and West Germany as major forces. In significantly different degrees in 'East' and 'West', but everywhere to some extent, old national forms have persisted and continue to command the loyalty of majorities, though also in every such nation, including those of 'the West', there is a significant minority who are conscious agents of the interests of the dominant power in the military alliance.

At the same time, in ways that Orwell could not have foreseen, these elements of political autonomy and diversity – within very narrow margins in the Warsaw Pact, within broader margins in NATO which contains most kinds of political state from liberal democracies to military dictatorships – are radically qualified by the nature of modern nuclear-weapons systems. The atomic war of *Nineteen Eighty-Four* is damaging but not disastrous; in fact it is made to precipitate the 'perpetual limited war' which is a central condition of the novel, in which the super-states are unconquerable because their rulers cannot risk atomic war. The war actually being fought, with its distant battles and its occasional rockets, belongs technologically to the 1940s. But then it is not only that the effects of atomic war have been underestimated; it is that the military and political consequences of a relative monopoly of nuclear weapons have turned out to be quite different from anything that Orwell and most others supposed.

Suppose – and really this is the likeliest development – that the surviving great nations make a tacit
agreement never to use the atomic bomb against
one another? Suppose they only use it, or the threat
of it, against people who are unable to retaliate? In
that case we are back where we were before, the
only difference being that power is concentrated in
still fewer hands and that the outlook for subject
peoples and oppressed classes is still more
hopeless. (CEJL, IV, 8)

Between the powers that have acquired atomic
weapons there has been neither formal nor tacit
agreement never to use the weapons against one
another. On the contrary, the predominant policy has
been one of mutual threat. Within this policy there has
not, as Orwell thought, been technical stagnation, but
a continual enlargement and escalation of weapons
systems, each typically developed under an alleged
threat of the superiority of the other side. And these
have now reached the point at which national autonomies, within the alliances, contradict in one central
respect the technical requirements of the most
modern systems, which require instant response or
even, some argue, preventive first use, if the other
power is not to gain an early and overwhelming
advantage.

It would be easy to argue from this, yet again, that
the Burnham/Orwell kind of super-state, with the
necessary unitary command, is inevitable, as a
product of the new weapons. But to move to that kind
of super-state, for all its strategic advantages, would
be to provoke major political problems – especially, for
example, in Western Europe – which would endanger

and probably break the now fragile compromise between surviving political autonomies and loyalties and the military-strategic alliance which has been superimposed on them. Thus Britain, in 1984, both is and is not, in Orwell's phrase, Airstrip One. It is dense with its own and foreign air and missile bases but it is also – and crucially, by a majority, is valued as – an independent political nation. To force the question to the point where it would have to be one thing *or* the other would bring into play all the forces which Orwell recognised in his essays but excluded from the novel. For the agents of paranational military and economic planning Britain has become, in a true example of Newspeak, the UK or Yookay. But for the peoples who live on the actual island there are more real and more valued names and relationships and considerations.

It is in the exclusion of even these traditional elements of resistance to what might seem a logical new order that Orwell, in the novel though usually not in the essays, went most obviously wrong. But there is an even larger error in the exclusion of new forces of resistance: most notably the national-liberation and revolutionary movements of what he knew as the colonial world. The monopoly of nuclear weapons, in the major industrialised states, has not prevented major advances towards autonomy among the 'subject peoples' whose condition he predicted as more hopeless. This is the peculiar unreality of the projection, that the old world powers, newly grouped into super-states, are seen as wholly dominant, and that the rest of the world is merely a passive quarry of minerals and cheap labour. Again, however, what has actually happened is complex. There have been political liberations in this vast area that Orwell reduced to passivity, but there is a limited sense in which what he foresaw has happened: not in super-state wars for its control, but in a complex of economic interventions, by paranational corporations which have some of the technical attributes of super-states; of political interventions, manoeuvres and 'destabilisations'; of exceptionally heavy arms exports to what in the worst cases become client states; and of military interventions, in some cases, where heavy and bloody fighting still excludes the use or threat of use of the nuclear weapons which in the perspective of the 1940s had seemed decisive for either conquest or blackmail.

Thus there has been, in one sense, the 'perpetual war' that Orwell thought likely, but it has been neither of a total nor of a phoney kind. The complex political and economic forces actually engaged have prevented the realisation of the apparently simple extrapolations from technical necessity or political ambition. It is sometimes hard to say, at this world-political level, whether the real 1984 is better or worse than the projected Nineteen Eighty-Four. It is more complex, more dynamic, more uncertain than the singular nightmare. Many more people are free or relatively free than the projection allowed, but also many more people have died or are dying in continuing 'small' wars, and vastly more live in danger of annihilation by nuclear war. The rationed and manipulated shortages of the projection have been succeeded by an extraordinary affluence in the privileged nations, and by actual and potential starvation in extending areas of the poor world. It is then not for showing danger and horror that anyone can reproach Orwell. If there is to be reproach, it is for looking so intently in one direction, with its simplified and easily dramatised dangers, that there is an excuse for not looking at other forces and developments which may, in the end, prove to be even more disastrous.

III

War is Peace is one notable chapter of the Book. As a comment on a perpetual and normalised *state* of war its details may be wrong but its feeling is right. 'We are the peace movement,' a British Government minister said recently, supporting the next phase of rearmament.

Ignorance is Strength is the other main chapter. This eventually describes the purposes and methods of thought control, but it begins with an analysis of the social structure of the super-states, based on a sort of historical-political theory:

> Throughout recorded time, and probably since the end of the Neolithic Age, there have been three kinds of people in the world, the High, the Middle and the Low. They have been subdivided in many ways, they have borne countless different names, and their relative numbers, as well as their attitude towards one another, have varied from age to age: but the essential structure of society has never altered. Even after enormous upheavals and seemingly irrevocable changes, the same pattern has always reasserted itself ... (NEF, 206-7)

It is at points like this that the status of the Book, in relation to Orwell's own thinking, is most problematic. Many examples could be quoted to show that he understood history as change rather than this abstract recurrence. The point is relevant again when the Book asserts:

> No advance in wealth, no softening of manners, no reform or revolution has ever brought human equality a millimetre nearer. (NEF, 208)

This is, as written, such obvious nonsense that the status of the whole argument becomes questionable. If this were really true, there would be no basis for calling Ingsoc a 'perversion'; it would be yet one more example of an inevitable, even innate process.

Clearly Orwell did not believe this, and neither did the author or the authors of the Book, a page or two on. For what is there argued is that while in earlier periods, because of the stage of development of the means of production, 'inequality was the price of civilisation', in the twentieth century 'human equality had become technically possible' with the development of 'machine production'. However, just at that point, 'all the main currents of political thought' stopped believing in equality and became authoritarian.

This level of argument is so perverse that one could indeed believe that O'Brien had written it. But more significantly it is an imperfect composition of three incompatible kinds of argument: one from Orwell, one from Burnham and one from Marx. The Marxist proposition of the unavoidable relations between the stages of development of the means of production and the formation of class societies, with the orthodox communist gloss that fully developed machine production would at last make equality possible, is unmistakably present. The Orwell argument or reservation that much talk of this kind, among its actual representatives, is just a cover for a new authoritarian conspiracy, ending capitalism but then even more thoroughly repressing and controlling the working class, is also evident. But the really discordant element, though it becomes dominant, is from Burnham. As Orwell summarises him in the first essay:

> Every great social movement, every war, every revolution, every political programme, however edifying and Utopian, really has behind it the ambitions of some sectional group which is out to grab power for itself ... So that history consists of a series of swindles, in which the masses are first lured into revolt by the promises of Utopia, and then, when they have done their job, enslaved over again by new masters. (CEJL, IV, 176–7)

In the essay Orwell circles hesitantly and intelligently around these crude propositions. He even comments:

> He ... assumes that the division of society into classes serves the same purpose in all ages. This is practically to ignore the history of hundreds of years. (CEJL, IV, 177)

And he goes on from this to the Marxist proposition, repeated in the Book, on the relation of class society to methods of production.

At the level of Orwell's direct arguments, then, the eventual emphasis of the Book is a known simplification. But it is the combination of this simplification with his own, often reasonable, reservations and suspicions about socialists or nominal socialists who are really authoritarians which determines the social structure of *Nineteen Eighty-Four*. His own contribution is then more specific than Burnham's. Burnham had foreseen a 'managerial revolution'. As Orwell summarises:

> Capitalism is disappearing, but Socialism is not replacing it. What is now arising is a new kind of planned, centralised society which will be neither capitalist nor, in any accepted sense of the word, democratic. The rulers of this new society will be the people who effectively control the means of production: that is, business executives, technicians, bureaucrats and soldiers, lumped together by Burnham under the name of 'managers'. These people will eliminate the old capitalist class, crush the working class, and so organise society that all power and economic privilege remain in their own hands. Private property rights will be abolished, but common ownership will not be established. (CEJL, IV, 160)

This is not, in any full sense, how things have actually turned out, though there are elements that are recognisable. But Orwell did not call the new social order Ingmana; he called it Ingsoc. Burnham's prediction, and the wider argument of which it is a relatively simple instance, pointed as clearly to Fascism and the Corporate State, or to what is now called a managed, interventionist post-capitalism, as to an authoritarian communism. It was Orwell who specialised it to a development within the socialist tradition, which it was also betraying. We can then, in 1984, only properly assess the prediction if we pull back to its full context.

In one way it is easy to understand Orwell's narrowing specialisation. Fascism, when he was writing, had just been militarily defeated. Capitalism, he assumed, was finished and deserved to be finished. What then mattered was which kind of socialism would come through, and since his option was for democratic socialism what he had mainly and even exclusively to oppose was authoritarian socialism.

> The real question is not whether the people who wipe their boots on us during the next fifty years are to be called managers, bureaucrats or politicians: the question is whether capitalism, now obviously doomed, is to give way to oligarchy or to true democracy. (CEJL, IV, 165)

This makes strange reading in 1984, especially if *Nineteen Eighty-Four* is there to tell us to concentrate our attention on Ingsoc and the Party. It is true that within the countries of what is now called 'actually existing socialism' this is broadly how it has turned out. Indeed the only correction we have to make, in that area, is that 'the Party', in that singular ideological sense, has proved to be less significant than the actual combination of technicians, bureaucrats and soldiers which the political monopoly of the Party makes possible and legitimises. It was significant during the Solidarity crisis in Poland that the different fractions of this hitherto effective ruling group were shown, under pressure, to have crucially variable interests, and more generally the idea of the monolithic Party has been shown to be false by a continuing series of internal dissensions and conflicts. However, that 'actually existing socialism' is still the prime case (though closely followed by the 'nationalised' or 'publicly owned' industries of the capitalist democracies) of the prediction that 'private property rights will be abolished, but common ownership will not be established'.

This does not mean, however, that the Orwell prediction of oligarchy has to be specialised, as in the novel, to 'Oligarchical Collectivism'. There are and for a long time have been many other forms of oligarchy. The most important modern form depends on the centralisation of effective political and economic controls. This has been associated with state versions of socialism, and indeed, ironically, Orwell conceded and approved this association:

> Centralised control is a necessary pre-condition of Socialism, but it no more produces Socialism than my typewriter would of itself produce this article I am writing. (CEJL, IV, 18)

But so far from this idea of a centralised socialism being a modern perversion, or likely to lead to it, it is in fact an old kind of socialism, of the period of the Fabians as much as of the Bolsheviks, and it has been increasingly rather than decreasingly challenged by new socialist ideas of decentralised politics and economic self-management. Orwell, in that sense, is behind even his own time.

Yet this is still to specialise the argument about oligarchy to socialism, when what has really undermined the basis of Orwell's prediction has been the phenomenal recovery of capitalism, which he had seen as 'doomed'. The spectacular capitalist boom from the mid-1950s to the early 1970s falsified virtually every element of the specific prediction. The real standard of living rose for many millions of working people. The main socialist movements, in the old industrial societies, moved steadily towards a consensus with the new, affluent, managed capitalism. Political liberties were not further suppressed, though their exercise became more expensive. The main motor of the boom, in an extraordinary expansion of consumer credit, was a new predominance of financial institutions, which gained in power at the expense of both political and industrial forces. When the boom ended, in depression and the return of mass unemployment, a new oligarchy was plainly in view. The national and international monetary institutions, with their counterparts in the giant paranational corporations, had established a both practical and ideological dominance which so far from being shaken by the first decade of depression and unemployment was actually reinforced by it. These were the actual forces now 'wiping their boots on us', in the old industrial societies and the new ex-colonial countries alike. Internally and externally they had all the features of a true oligarchy, and a few people, at least, began to learn that 'centralisation' is not just an old socialist nostrum but is a practical process of ever-larger and more concentrated capitalist corporations and money markets. State power, meanwhile, though trying to withdraw from its earlier commitments to common provision for social welfare, has increased at military levels, in the new weapons systems, and in its definitions of law and order and of security (backed up by some intensive surveillance). Thus it is an obvious case of *doublethink* when the radical Right, now in power in so many countries, denounce the state at the level of social welfare or economic justice but reinforce and applaud the state at the level of patriotic militarism, uniform loyalty, and control over local democratic institutions. To hear some of the loudest of these double-mouthed people is to know what is meant, in Newspeak, by a *doubleplusgood duckspeaker*.

But then what about the *proles*? Here again the prediction was quite wrong, though there are a few disillusioned people thinking it might have been right. For the key feature of the new capitalist oligarchy is that it has not left 'eighty-five per cent of the population' to their own devices. On the contrary, it has successfully organised most of them as a market, calling them now not 'proles' but 'consumers' (the two terms are equally degrading). It is true that there is massive provision, by the newspapers and other media of the oligarchy, of the semi-pornography and gambling and mechanical fiction which the Party was supposed to provide. (This, incidentally, is one of Orwell's interesting errors about Soviet communism, where the Party has exercised its ideological controls *against* these mainly 'Western' phenomena.) But the real controls are different. A straight contract between disciplined wage-labour and credit-financed consumption was offered and widely accepted. Even as it became unavailable to the many millions who in depression became, in that cruel oligarchic term, 'redundant', its social and political hold, as the essence of any social order, was at first barely disturbed. Indeed the ideological response of the oligarchy was to act to make the contract more secure: by disciplining the trade unions which represent an independent element in its bargaining, beyond oligarchic control; and by identifying as public enemies, in its newspapers, dissenting political figures: not the 'proper official Opposition' but the 'unofficial' Reds, Wreckers, Extremists, who in good *Nineteen Eighty-Four* style are seen as either mad or guilty of *thoughtcrime*.

IV

It would be surprising if one kind of oligarchy could succeed, for long, in using the features of another to distract attention from its own. Yet *Nineteen Eighty-Four*, in 1984, is being primarily used for just this purpose, ironically by some of the same propaganda methods which it exposes and attacks. Because what Orwell wanted to show as a universal tendency became attached (by his choice, though he protested against it) to the practice of socialism, any anti-socialist movement can exploit it, even in ways which confirm its own deepest warnings. It is one thing for dissident and oppositional groups in Eastern Europe to say, as some of them do, that *Nineteen Eighty-Four* shows the underlying truth of their condition. I was asked by students, in one communist country, to lecture on Orwell, and I did so willingly, against some official disapproval, because I wanted to follow the whole argument through: not just what could be mocked or hated but what could still, genuinely, be believed. Beyond the obvious pyrotechnics of the projection there is, however qualified, a steady insistence on the value of thinking for oneself and of refusing the official simplifications which all ruling groups employ. The more there is to be mocked or hated, in any system, the more it is necessary to resist these feelings being used by others, for their own governing purposes. One scene in the novel sticks in my mind, in this later period, when the figurehead of the Opposition, Goldstein, appears on the screen –

> demanding the immediate conclusion of peace with Eurasia . . . advocating freedom of speech, freedom of the Press, freedom of assembly, freedom of thought . . . And all the while, lest one should be in any doubt as to the reality which Goldstein's specious claptrap covered, behind his head on the telescreen marched the endless columns of the Eurasian army . . . (NEF, 16)

This trick is now being played so often: certainly in official denunciations of unofficial peace, civil rights and workers' movements in Eastern Europe as 'Western-inspired'; but just as certainly in the West, as when the independent peace movements are directly accused of serving Russian interests, 'the endless columns of the Eurasian army'. Meanwhile anyone can see that the other side's Big Brother is a tyrant and a fraud, but the endlessly imposed ruling faces of one's own side are supposed indeed to be 'loved'.

It is interesting that what has really survived, from *Nineteen Eighty-Four*, is Orwell's understanding of propaganda and thought control. There have been changes of style and technology but certain basic methods of the oligarchy – endlessly repeated slogans, displacements of one kind of news by another, the regular institution of hate-figures – are still clearly recognisable. In 1946 Orwell wrote:

> In England the immediate enemies of truthfulness, and hence of freedom of thought, are the press lords, the film magnates, and the bureaucrats. (CEJL, IV, 64)

That familiar case still holds. But there is another key element in Orwell's diagnosis:

> But ... on a long view the weakening of the desire for liberty among the intellectuals themselves is the most serious symptom of all. (CEJL, IV, 64)

It was from this conviction that some of the most specific features of *Nineteen Eighty-Four* were composed. In a way what is most surprising about its tyrannical system is that it more or less neglects eighty-five per cent of the population and is concerned mainly with controlling the thoughts and the very memories of a minority.

It is difficult to follow this kind of anticipation through. There are no obvious objective events from which to assess it. But I have sometimes felt that almost the exact opposite has happened. I do not mean that there have not been time-serving and even lying 'intellectuals', together with a much larger executive group with conveniently selective memories. I mean that there is a case for saying that in the capitalist democracies there has been intense and continuous attention to the state of mind of the eighty-five per cent (or whatever the precise figure for majority popular opinion might be) and a relative indifference to what 'intellectuals' – already marked off as peculiar – believe or do. It is different, I know, in the 'actually existing socialist' societies, where there

Totalitarianism

has been intense pressure, and worse, on just these minority groups. It can be reasonably argued that because the capitalist societies are electoral democracies attention to majorities is inevitable, while minorities can be disregarded and even sneered at or, obscurely, shown to be 'wrong' *because* they are minorities. Yet, beyond this difference of systems, and even after allowing for the fact that Orwell was parodying monolithic one-party societies, it is still the case that he thought that the state of mind of intellectuals would be decisive. And then there is indeed some basis for saying that we could wish that he had been right.

The point bears most closely on the notorious 'memory hole'. For if there is one thing that has not proved necessary, in manipulating majority opinion, it is systematically rewriting the past. On the contrary, the past in itself becomes a kind of memory hole, from which only a few scholars and researchers bother to uncover and recover the facts. Why were the first atom bombs dropped on Japan *after* its government had proposed the outline of a peace? What really happened in the Gulf of Tonkin? Which way and during what peace negotiations was the *General Belgrano* sailing? These are questions (none, in their whole context, with very simple answers) which with a thousand others, from the role of Trotsky in the Russian Revolution to the policy of Mao and the Red Guards in China, are still intensely inquired into by small minorities, while the dominant public stance, in one social order after another, is to go blithely on with the news of the day, leaving the past to the obsessive and to the dry-as-dust. General versions of the past, selected and packaged to show the present as inevitable and the ruling future as desirable, are of course deployed. But the detail, the two-and-two of the inquiry, can be there and not there: in the books and the monographs and the seminars but not in what is aggressively presented as 'the real world'. Orwell was right, of course, to attack the time-serving, submissive and lying intellectuals whom he had encountered and saw proliferating. But in *Nineteen Eighty-Four* there is another level, quite contrary to his own best practice, in which the scheming and the power-hungry are of this intellectual kind, and the only actual alternative to them are the stupid and ignorant, protected by stupidity and ignorance. And what then of the Party slogan, *Ignorance is Strength*?

It has not, on any reckoning, worked out like that. This is especially the case in what he saw as the worst danger: power-worship. There has been plenty of that, but not just from some intellectual habit. Militarism, chauvinism, tough policing, penal cruelty have been general epidemics. And the people in charge of them, in any social order, have not needed intellectuals to justify what they are doing, though in some systems they take care to employ hacks. The powerful and the fraudulent have been the powerful and the fraudulent. Their interests are their reasons; they do not need cogitators.

But this brings us to the hardest question in a reassessment of *Nineteen Eighty-Four*. Worried and fascinated by Burnham's arguments that power is the only political reality, whatever phrases may accompany it, Orwell observed:

It is curious that in all his talk about the struggle for power, Burnham never stops to ask *why* people

want power. He seems to assume that power
hunger, although only dominant in comparatively
few people, is a natural instinct that does not have to
be explained. (CEJL, IV, 177)

It is fascinating that when Winston Smith comes to the
point in his reading of the Book when this motive to
power is to be explained he realises that Julia has been
asleep for some time and puts the book away, still
wondering what the secret could be. The question
returns only during his torture by O'Brien, and
O'Brien answers it:

The object of persecution is persecution. The object
of torture is torture. The object of power is power.
Now do you begin to understand me? (NEF, 269)

'A natural instinct that does not have to be explained'?
This is the terrifying irrationalism of the climax of
Nineteen Eighty-Four, and it is not easy, within the pity
and the terror, to persist with the real and Orwell's
own question. The point of Burnham's position is to
discredit all actual political beliefs and aspirations,
since these are invariably covers for naked power or
the wish for it. But if this is so, there is not only a
cancellation of history – as Orwell in his essay went on
to observe. The real variations of what happened, as
well as of what was said and believed, are flattened
into a meaningless, degrading uniformity of human
action. There is also a cancellation of inquiry and
argument, and therefore of the possibility of truth,
since whatever is said can be instantly translated into
the base and cruel reality which it is known to cover. It
is not necessary to deny the existence, even the fre-

quent occurrence, of persecution and power and torture 'for their own sake' (meaning, for the private gratification of their executors, rather than for any objective cause) to go on resisting the cancellation of all links between power and policy. And this cancellation *must* be resisted, if only because it would then be pointless to try to distinguish between social systems, or to inquire, discriminatingly, where this or that system went good or went bad.

There is plenty of room for disagreement about the social and political systems which make arbitrary power, persecution and torture more or less likely. In the world of the actual 1984 there is so vast an extent of these practices, in social systems otherwise dissimilar – from Chile to Kampuchea, from Turkey and El Salvador to Eastern Europe, and with instances from as close to home as Belfast – that it is tempting to override the discriminating questions, to recoil from man become brute. Yet it is the two-plus-two kind of reckoning – obstinately factual and truthful, however complex the sums may become – that is then most at risk. There *are* reasons, as outside the fiction Orwell well knew, why there are systems and phases of systems in which, as throughout recorded history, opponents and even inconvenients are imprisoned, tortured and killed; just as there are other systems and phases of systems – nearly all of them modern; nearly all of them achieved by prolonged political argument and struggle – when these brutal short-cuts are lessened or brought under control. Of course Orwell is warning against a modern totalitarian system, developed beyond even Stalin or Hitler. But there is a totalitarian way of warning against totalitarianism, by excluding just those discriminating historical analyses, those veridical political distinctions, those authentic as distinct from assumed beliefs and aspirations, which are a much better protection against it than the irrational projection inspiring either terror or hate. It is useful to remember what he said of Burnham:

> Burnham is trying to build up a picture of terrifying, irresistible power, and to turn a normal political manoeuvre like infiltration into Infiltration adds to the general portentousness. (CEJL, IV, 170)

It can be the same with Ingsoc. As he again said in discussing Burnham's thesis:

> Power worship blurs political judgment because it leads, almost unavoidably, to the belief that present trends will continue. (CEJL, IV, 174)

Yet Orwell himself, always an opponent of privilege and power, committed himself, in the fiction, to just that submissive belief. The warning that the world could be going that way became, in the very absoluteness of the fiction, an imaginative submission to its inevitability. And then to rattle that chain again is to show little respect to those many men and women, including from the whole record Orwell himself, who have fought and are fighting the destructive and ignorant trends that are still so powerful, and who have kept the strength to imagine, as well as to work for, human dignity, freedom and peace.

Booklist, References, Acknowledgements

Books by Orwell
DOPL   : *Down and Out in Paris and London;* London, 1933
BD   : *Burmese Days;* New York, 1934
CD   : *A Clergyman's Daughter;* London, 1935
KAF   : *Keep the Aspidistra Flying;* London, 1936
RWP   : *The Road to Wigan Pier;* London, 1937
HC   : *Homage to Catalonia;* London, 1938
CUA   : *Coming Up For Air;* London, 1939
IW   : *Inside the Whale;* London, 1940
AF   : *Animal Farm;* London, 1945
NEF   : *Nineteen Eighty-Four;* London, 1949
CEJL   : *Collected Essays, Journalism and Letters of George Orwell;* 4 volumes, edited by Sonia Orwell and Ian Angus; London, 1968

Page references, other than CEJL, are to the Uniform Edition. Acknowledgement of copyright in quotations to Sonia Brownell Orwell and to Secker and Warburg Limited, 14 Carlisle Street, London, W1. All books by Orwell mentioned above are available in Penguin paperback editions.

Some Books about Orwell
Aldrith, Keith *The Making of George Orwell*. London, Edward Arnold, 1969
Atkins, John *George Orwell*. London, Calder, 1954
Brander, Laurence *George Orwell*. London, Longman, 1954
Calder, Jennie *Chronicles of Conscience* (part). London, Secker & Warburg, 1968

Crick, Bernard *George Orwell: a Life*. London, Secker & Warburg, 1980

Greenblatt, S. J. *Three Modern Satirists* (part). New Haven, Yale, 1965

Gross, M. (ed.) *The World of George Orwell*. London, Weidenfeld & Nicolson, 1971

Hollis, Christopher *A Study of George Orwell*. London, Hollis & Carter, 1958

Lee, Robert A. *Orwell's Fiction*. Notre Dame, Indiana, 1969

Lief, Ruth A. *Homage to Oceania*. Ohio State University, 1969

Oxley, B. *George Orwell*. London, Evans, 1967

Rees, Richard *George Orwell–Fugitive from the Camp of Victory*. London, Secker & Warburg, 1961

Stansky, P. and Abrahams, W. *The Unknown Orwell*. London, Constable, 1972

Thomas, Edward M. *Orwell*. Edinburgh, Oliver & Boyd, 1953

Vorhees, Richard J. *The Paradox of George Orwell*. Lafayette, Indiana, Purdue University, 1961

Williams, R. (ed.) *Twentieth Century Views: George Orwell*. New Jersey, Prentice-Hall, 1974

Willison, J. R. *George Orwell: Some Materials for a Bibliography*. School of Librarianship and Archives, University of London

Woodcock, George *The Crystal Spirit*. London, Cape, 1967